A MEMOIR

NOBU

NOBU

A MEMOIR

Nobuyuki Matsuhisa

EMILY BESTLER BOOKS
—
ATRIA

New York London Toronto Sydney New Delhi

EMILY
BESTLER
BOOKS

ATRIA

An Imprint of Simon & Schuster, Inc.
1230 Avenue of the Americas
New York, NY 10020

Copyright © 2014 by Nobuyuki Matsuhisa

English language translation copyright © 2017 by Cathy Hirano

Originally published in Japanese in 2014 by Diamond Inc. as
The Smiling Faces of My Guests Mean Everything

First Emily Bestler Books/Atria Books hardcover edition November 2017

EMILY BESTLER BOOKS / ATRIA BOOKS and colophons are trademarks of Simon & Schuster, Inc.

For information about special discounts for bulk purchases, please contact Simon & Schuster Special Sales at 1-866-506-1949 or business@simonandschuster.com

The Simon & Schuster Speakers Bureau can bring authors to your live event. For more information or to book an event, contact the Simon & Schuster Speakers Bureau at 1-866-248-3049 or visit our website at www.simonspeakers.com.

Interior design by Amy Trombat

Manufactured in the United States of America

10 9 8 7 6 5 4 3 2 1

Library of Congress Cataloging-in-Publication Data
Names: Matsuhisa, Nobuyuki, author.
Title: Nobu : a memoir / by Nobuyuki Matsuhisa.
Other titles: Smiling faces of my guests mean everything. English
Description: New York : Atria, [2017] | "Emily Bestler Books." | "Originally
   published in Japanese in 2014 by Diamond Publishing as The Smiling Faces
   of My Guests Mean Everything."
Identifiers: LCCN 2017024524 (print) | LCCN 2017026295 (ebook) |
Subjects: LCSH: Matsuhisa, Nobuyuki. | Restaurateurs—Japan—Biography. |
   Restaurateurs—United States—Biography.
Classification: LCC TX910.5.M344 (ebook) | LCC TX910.5.M344 A3 2017 (print) |
   DDC 647.95092 [B]—dc23
LC record available at https://lccn.loc.gov/2017024524

ISBN 978-1-5011-2279-8
ISBN 978-1-5011-2281-1 (ebook)

Contents

2
Once You've Hit Rock Bottom, Impatience Vanishes   27
A series of failures in foreign lands

3
A Place Filled with the Laughter of My Guests   53
Launching Matsuhisa, my first restaurant

4
Robert De Niro, the Man Who Waited Four Years   83
The beginning of the Nobu management team

5
Conveying the Taste and Service of Nobu to the World   103
What to keep and what to adapt to the locality

6

Transcending a Crisis in Our Partnership 129
Constantly perfecting quality

7
Heading into a New Stage   155
Launching Nobu Hotel

8
Work Hard with Passion.
The Rest Will Come.   179

Afterword   201

Preface

—

To See My Guests Smile

I entered the world of cooking as an apprentice chef at a sushi bar in Shinjuku when I was just seventeen. At the time, I never imagined that one day I would run over thirty restaurants and hotels on five continents.

People often ask me for the secret of my success or my method for succeeding globally, but I have never thought of myself as "succeeding." Quite frankly, I'm still learning, and I don't believe that there is any golden rule that guarantees success. I simply threw myself into my work and did my best to do the right thing.

In my business, that means choosing the best ingredients, caring about my guests, putting my heart into my cooking because I want to please them, and offering dishes at a price that matches the quality of the food. If you consistently offer good food and good service, your guests will always come back. To me, the "right thing" means constantly repeating this process.

The restaurants that bear my name, Nobu, are considered high end, but they're not exclusive. Families with small children are welcome at all Nobu locations except those in luxury hotels. I want Nobu to bring smiles to our guests' faces with the first bite of food, to give them a place to relax, enjoy good conversation over a great meal, and leave happy. And I constantly encourage our team to strive for this goal.

Nobu originated with Matsuhisa in Los Angeles, my very first restaurant. It was nothing special—just a little thirty-eight-seat establishment that was later expanded to sixty-five seats. Nobu's roots can be traced back even further to Matsuei-sushi, the sushi bar in Shinjuku where I spent my years as an apprentice.

Sushi is a simple dish that is prepared right before the guest. The ingredients are just fish and rice; the tools, a knife and ten fingers. The heart of the sushi chef communicates directly to the guest. It's impossible to fake it. Or to cut corners. Even the smallest of actions must never become "routine." I must put my heart and soul into everything I do. This dedication, this passion, is the essence of Nobu. Size makes no difference. Whether it's a restaurant that seats 38 or 374, I treat every guest as though each meal is a once-in-a-lifetime occasion.

Collecting Michelin stars is not my aim. All I want is to see my guests smile. For me, the greatest happiness, the highest honor, is to please my guests. So I try to imagine what I might want if I were them and spare no effort to provide it. If there is any key to global "success" in what I do, perhaps it is this simple approach. And I'll keep on going this way, moving forward little by little, without pausing or rushing, always mindful of my roots.

Along the way, I have faced some major stumbling blocks. But each time, I have managed to overcome them. Whenever I hit an obstacle, I search for a solution and carry on. Gradually, the hurdles that appear before me have become smaller. I find that if I plow ahead, no matter how impossible that may seem, and just do my best, someone is bound to lend a hand. Keep moving forward, even if it's just a millimeter a day. That's my motto.

I went through a lot before I reached this place: the death of my father, getting expelled from high school, years spent working my way up from the bottom rung, anger and frustration in Peru, discouragement in Argentina, and a setback in Alaska that was so severe I contemplated suicide . . . I hope that the lessons I have learned through these experiences will inspire those who long to pursue their dreams.

Drawn to Foreign Lands and Sushi

—

Thanks to my years as an apprentice

LONGING TO TRAVEL LIKE MY FATHER

I don't remember my childhood in much detail. Instead, fragmented images flash through my mind.

My father ran a lumber business in Sugito, a town in Saitama Prefecture. Sometimes he went overseas to buy lumber. He must have been a busy man. The last of his four children, I have almost no memories of playing with him. What I do remember is the warmth of his back when I rode behind him on his motorcycle. He often took me with him when he went places for work. It was the 1950s, and much of Saitama remained undeveloped. I loved speeding through the beautiful countryside, slicing through the wind while clinging to the back of this man whom I admired so much.

One day, I returned home from school to find my father about to leave. I held on to the back of his motorcycle and insisted that he take me, too. I must have really pestered him, because I remember that someone finally took a photo of us together, my father astride the bike and me standing on the back with my hands on his shoulders. But my father said he was going too far to take me with him and left alone. I can still see his back receding into the distance . . . It was a June afternoon, just two months after I began elementary school.

The next image is of my father in a hospital bed, covered in blood and groaning in pain. He'd been in an accident. This scene is followed by one of his funeral. Many relatives were there.

My memories jump like this from one scene to another.

Never again would I cling to my father's back and ride through the wind. Never again would he hoist me onto his shoulders. Never again would we play catch together. I think it took some time for this to sink in.

I was so jealous when I saw my friends riding on their fathers' shoulders or playing catch together. Sometimes I felt lonely, wondering why my father had to die. At those times, I would look at his photo. In it, he's standing in front of what looks like a palm tree. Beside him is a local man dressed only in a loincloth. Later, I learned that this photo was taken during the Second World War when my father went to Palau to buy lauan wood. In those days, few Japanese civilians traveled overseas on business. I was very proud of him for traveling all alone to unexplored territory. And I felt the pull of distant lands myself. "When I grow up, I want to go overseas just like my father," I thought. That was my first dream.

INHERITING MY GRANDMOTHER'S FIGHTING SPIRIT

The Matsuhisa family had lost its main breadwinner. My mother must have been at a complete loss when my father died so suddenly. Although she had helped him with his work, she didn't even know the price of the company's products. Once I remember her saying, "Your father came to see me last night." Perhaps she had dreamed of him.

The customers demanded to know what she was going to do. She consulted my eldest brother, Noboru, who was then in grade twelve, but my second-eldest brother, Keiichi, intervened. "Let him graduate from high school," he said. "I'll take a year off." He helped my mother until Noboru graduated the following spring and then reenrolled in grade ten while Noboru took over the company.

Noboru's grades were good, and he had planned to go on to university and become a doctor. My father's death, however, meant that he had to give up this dream. For a while, he became quite sullen and angry, perhaps due to the stress. Sometimes he drank and vented his frustration on my mother. In retrospect, I can see how hard it must have been for both of them.

Because of our situation, I spent most of my time with my grandmother. Born in the Meiji era (1868–1912), a time of great social upheaval in Japan, she was strong-willed and an avid pro wrestling fan. Rikidozan was her favorite wrestler. One day, I got into a fight and came home crying. She scolded me, but not for fighting or for crying. In those days, schoolboys still wore *geta*, or heavy wooden sandals. "Why did you come back with your *geta* on?" she demanded. "If they made you mad enough to cry, at least throw your *geta* at them before coming home!" Perhaps it's from her that I inherited my fighting spirit, which forces me back on my feet whenever I fall.

THE DAY I DECIDED TO BECOME A SUSHI CHEF

When I was a child, I slept near the kitchen. I would wake every morning to the tap-tap of the knife on the cutting board, the scraping of the pot against the burner, the sound of water gushing from the kitchen faucet, and the savory aroma of soup stock and miso as my mother made soup. She was the old-fashioned type of housewife who kneaded the fermented rice bran in the pickling crock every day. She was a good cook, too. Although not the type to make elaborate, time-consuming dishes, she could whip up a meal without wasting time and effort, using whatever ingredients

The photo of my father that I always looked at as a child.

happened to be on hand. It made her happy to see us enjoy her cooking. She must have been incredibly busy, juggling both the business and the housework, but mealtime when I was a boy was fun. My first memories of food come from the joy of our family gathered around the dinner table.

One day, my eldest brother, Noboru, took me to Uokou, a sushi bar in front of the local train station. It must have been when I was still in junior high school. Back then, sushi was a special treat ordered in for guests, and we would be lucky to get any that was left over. There was no such thing as conveyor belt sushi, and going to a sushi restaurant was extra special. I expect that I behaved like a spoiled brat and insisted that Noboru take me. He ducked under the *noren* (shop curtain) and slid open the door. I peered around him to see inside. The sushi chefs behind the counter called out, *"Irasshai!"* (meaning "welcome"). I felt very nervous, as if I were sneaking into an adult world where kids didn't belong. Yet, at the same time, I was spellbound by the microcosm of the sushi bar into which I had stepped for the first time in my life.

Seeing how nervous I was, Noboru ordered for me. The distinctive fragrance of vinegared rice and the swift, unerring movements of the chefs captivated me. *"Toro, gyoku, shako, agari, sabi . . ."* I hadn't a clue what they were saying, but the sound of the words that flew back and forth made my heart sing. Then, pieces of sushi, made especially for me, were placed on the counter, and I popped them in my mouth. They were really and truly delicious.

The restaurant, the movements of the sushi chefs, the exchanges across the counter, the conversations among the customers themselves, the sheen of the sushi toppings, the aroma of sushi rice . . . It was all the coolest thing ever. I decided then and there that I wanted to become a sushi chef. This became my second dream.

Before that, I had been drawn to such professions as gym teacher or soldier in the Self-Defense Forces. These worlds seemed dynamic and disciplined. Actually, I now see that they share something in common with the precise movements of a sushi chef. Those were the kinds of things that attracted me when I was young. But although I was drawn to foreign lands and sushi, it did not yet occur to me to choose a path in life that would fulfill those dreams. I had been born into the lumber business and, just like Keiichi, my second-eldest brother, I went on to Omiya Technical High School. There I joined the boys' cheerleading squad. Again, I think I chose it because I loved dynamic action.

DRIVING WITHOUT A LICENSE AND GETTING EXPELLED FROM SCHOOL

I fell in with the wrong crowd in my hometown. When I was in eleventh grade, a gang of friends gathered at my house the night before our end-of-term exams. Supposedly, we were going to study, but once everyone else in the house was asleep, we decided to take Keiichi's car out for a spin. I snuck the key from his room and started the engine. Of course, none of us had a license to drive.

I got behind the wheel and drove out onto National Route 4. It was the middle of the night, but there was more traffic than I had expected. It was 1963, the year before the first Tokyo Olympics, and construction was booming in Tokyo. Dump trucks zoomed back and forth day and night. There is nothing scarier than a cocky driver without a license. I pulled out and passed one truck after another. But when I tried to pass one more, I slammed into a car coming from the opposite direction. Our vehicle flipped and then rolled several times before it was hit by another car.

Ambulances and police cars soon arrived on the scene. At the sight of the damage, a policeman asked, "Where are the bodies?" My friends and I were shaking uncontrollably, certain that our lives were over. Amazingly, however, all of us, including me, were unscathed, and the people in the other vehicles had escaped with only minor injuries. It was nothing short of a miracle. The memory of that crash still sends shivers down my spine. I am convinced that my father protected us.

Since then I have had several other close shaves that make me shudder, experiences where one wrong move would have ended my life. Yet each time, some invisible power has saved me in ways that can only be described as miraculous. And each time, I have felt that my father was watching out for me.

I used to talk to my father's photo when things weren't going well, especially when I was younger. To be honest, I spent most of my time complaining rather than praying to him. "Why'd you have to go and die?" I would say. "Why aren't you here to help me now when things are so rough?" As I talked, I would feel a weight lift from my chest. Recently, I have finally reached the stage where, instead of complaining, I place my palms together and thank him from the bottom of my heart. Perhaps it's a sign that I've finally grown up.

But to return to my story, the day after the accident, I didn't sit for the exams. Having been informed of what happened, the school understandably expelled me. They really had no choice considering that I had caused a major accident. To top it off, the court ordered that I was to be placed under probation until the age of twenty. My mother must have been worried sick, yet instead of reproaching me, she never mentioned the accident. I think the fact that she believed in me is what kept me from taking the wrong path. I began helping out with the family business instead of going to school, but my dream of becoming a sushi chef did not fade.

THREE YEARS OF WASHING DISHES AND DELIVERING SUSHI

I'm pretty sure that I consulted my mother or Noboru about my aspirations. The master of Uokou, the sushi bar in front of our local station where Noboru had once taken me, introduced me to the owner of a sushi bar in Shinjuku. As I had no way of judging which shop was a good one, I went where I was told. On June tenth, in my seventeenth year, I took my first step as an apprentice chef at Matsuei-sushi.

I had never lived away from home before, but now I shared one large room in the back of the restaurant with the two other staff. The sushi bar was closed just two days a month, and those were our only days off. Because we were live-in staff, there was a curfew. Even on our holidays, we had to be back by ten at night. The owner and his wife were quite strict about this, probably because I was underage and they felt responsible. My workday began early in the morning. Every day, I got on the bus with my boss and headed to the Tsukiji fish market. I followed after him with a basket to carry the fish he bought. I learned how to tell a good fish by watching him choose.

This was also a time of day when I could enjoy small acts of kindness. A vegetable broker might give me a bun to eat, or sometimes my boss would buy me something I could never have afforded. I still remember the times he treated me to eel or pork cutlet on curry and rice.

Back at the restaurant, it was time to prepare. For me, food prep consisted of the most basic tasks, such as scaling and beheading small fish. I was not particularly skillful with my hands. My only strength was my determination to keep up with the others. I couldn't stand being beaten even at such simple tasks as prepping shad or conger eel. The fishermen at Tsukiji market could dress a fish with a few fluid movements, and I often watched them while they worked, hoping to learn how they did it so quickly and efficiently.

Once prep work was done, my coworkers would start grilling eel, and the owner's wife would mix the sushi rice. Then it was lunch hour. When the sushi bar was open, I was stationed at the far end of the counter where I washed dishes, made tea, grated wasabi, and cut leaf garnishes. I also delivered takeout orders.

A COMBINATION PLATTER FOR BASEBALL STAR SADAHARU OH

Before I could start delivering orders on my own, I first had to learn where all the customers lived. One of them was homerun king Sadaharu Oh, who played for the Yomiuri Giants. My boss was a graduate of Waseda Jitsugyo High School and so was Oh. Through this connection, Oh had become a regular, and an autographed photo of him hung on the wall in the restaurant.

At the time, Oh was the main batter for the Giants but had not yet attained international fame. He wasn't married yet, either. When he finished a game at Korakuen Stadium, his mother would phone us and order "the usual for Sadaharu." Matsuei-sushi had a special combination platter of sushi and sashimi just for Oh. The boss would make it, and I would deliver it. Sometimes Oh would drive up just as I arrived, and I would direct him as he backed into the driveway.

Although I was nominally an apprentice sushi chef, I spent the first three years washing dishes and making deliveries. Some of my high school friends were now working, and they brought their girlfriends to the restaurant when they got their paychecks, but I had no skills with which to impress them. While I was happy that they had come especially to see me, I also felt a bit embarrassed.

Whenever I had a chance between tasks, I studied my boss and the other staff as they made sushi. I would roll up a small cloth, pretend it was sushi rice, and mimic their hand movements. On holidays, I would sometimes ask the boss for the leftover sushi rice so that I could practice. My days off, however, began with making the rounds of people who had ordered deliveries the previous day. I would collect the dishes and check that the money matched the orders. Then I tackled several days' worth of laundry. By then, it was usually evening. That was the only free time I had.

My boss lived with his wife, his mother, his two sons, and his daughter. Sometimes I was asked to take his youngest son to kindergarten or to pick him up afterwards. On days when the restaurant was closed, the boss's family would prepare their dinner in the evening. I remember seeing them sitting around the table enjoying a meal of sukiyaki, but my coworkers and I were not included in that circle. Perhaps I still remember because I envied them. And perhaps I was a bit lonely.

On days off, we had a few hours of freedom in the evening

after we finished doing all our chores. The other two went drinking, but being underage, I couldn't. Instead, I would go to the movies. There were many theaters near the restaurant, and I often got free tickets at the local public bath. Not having much money, I was very grateful for those tickets. I loved movies like A *Man from Abashiri Prison* starring Ken Takakura. Afterward, I would eat at a nearby cafeteria and then go home to sleep. That was the kind of life I led.

STICKING IT OUT MADE ME WHAT I AM TODAY

Live-in apprentices were guaranteed one thing only: a room. Initially, my wages were so low that I couldn't even buy myself a knife. I was dying to have one of my own, and a senior coworker gave me one of his that was broken. "Here," he said. "If you can fix it, it's yours."

I wasn't about to pass up this opportunity. I had some experience sharpening chisels and planes in the workshop at my family's business, and so I took it apart, then sharpened and reconstructed it. When I was done, I showed it to my coworker. "I did it!" I announced.

He took the knife and just said, "Thanks."

I wanted to accuse him of breaking his word, but the pecking order in the restaurant business was very strict, and I had to take it without complaining. This incident, however, fueled my fighting spirit, and I was determined to show him up by becoming better than him at whatever I did.

I also had to endure being on probation. As a minor who had caused a serious accident, I was required to visit the probation officer once a month until the age of twenty to have my probation book stamped. My boss and his wife, both of whom knew this, would give me permission to leave work early whenever the day for my visit came around. I walked the few blocks from our restaurant to the probation officer's house. My probation officer was a woman named Mrs. Yamada, and I had to report to her what I had done during the last month and have her stamp my book. I was still feeling defiant, and that probably showed in my attitude. Sometimes she would pop by the restaurant and look inside on her way somewhere. I could feel her eyes on me, and it hurt my pride to be under constant supervision. Although it was my own fault, I still found this hard to bear. Looking back on it, I'm just glad that I didn't give up.

I was so intent on proving to those who "spied" on me that they were wrong that I showed up faithfully every month to have my book stamped. These efforts were rewarded. My probation, which should have lasted until I reached maturity, was terminated after just one year. I was told that I didn't need to come anymore and given a necktie, five 100-yen coins, and a certificate. I shredded the certificate as well as the stamp book that I had used for the last year and slashed the tie into pieces with a pair of scissors. That's how immature I was, even though I was an apprentice sushi chef taking my first steps toward my goal.

But those years of persevering at the bottom of the pecking order and enduring the humiliation of constant supervision were a priceless period in my life. I had announced to one and all that I would become a sushi chef, and if I gave up, I would look like a fool. This knowledge drove me on. Having been expelled from school, nothing was going to make me deviate from this path, regardless of any wounds to my self-esteem. That, I think, is why I was able to stick it out to the end. To lose my temper would have meant the end of everything.

WORK FOR A FINE PERSON, NOT FOR A FINE SHOP

I later learned that if I had worked for a larger restaurant, I could have lived in a nice dorm. The master of Uokou, who had introduced me to Matsuei-sushi, had connections to some famous establishments. But he had introduced me to Matsuei-sushi instead because he believed that my boss's caring attitude was more important. "The master of that restaurant is a good man," he told me. Also, being as young as I was, I am not sure that I would have thrown myself so single-mindedly into my work if I had lived in a dorm with a lot of people my own age.

My mother must have been far more reassured to know that I

was working for a "fine man" rather than for a "fine shop." I now know that the character of the people who work at a restaurant is more important than its size or reputation. I would rather be known as a good man than for my restaurant to be known for making money. Even so, my mother must have been terribly worried. Yet she never stopped believing in me. This motivated me to keep on trying. When a child knows that his parent believes in him, he simply cannot betray that trust. Trust, not doubt. That, I believe, is the foundation of the bond between parent and child, as well as that between master and apprentice.

The owner of Matsuei-sushi was certainly under no obligation to take on a young delinquent as his apprentice, yet he believed in me and gave me a chance. I could not waste that opportunity. Once, I was sharpening a knife while watching TV and cut my finger so deeply that I still bear the scar to this day. I had failed to take that knife seriously. My boss was furious. "A knife is a weapon!" he shouted. "You could kill someone with it. Keep that in mind when you grip a knife in your hand, and give it your full attention." He drilled that lesson into me. Although he was very strict, he taught me the attitude appropriate to a professional who wields a knife.

AIM HIGH AND YOU WILL GROW

About three years after I started working at Matsuei-sushi, the coworker who had broken his promise to give me his knife quit, and I was promoted to the position of *oimawashi*, which meant that I now assisted the other coworker in his work as sushi chef. He would tell me to do this or that, and by following his instructions, I finally started learning how to do things. This made me very happy, because that was still the era when apprentices were expected to learn just by watching.

As I gradually became more capable, I was entrusted with more work; only small jobs, though, such as making *norimaki* rolls or *inarizushi* for people to take home. I had also managed to save some money despite my low wages because I spent very little with only two days off a month. A few years after I started my apprenticeship, Matsuei-sushi began closing for two days in a row every other month. I used these holidays as opportunities to travel with my best friend from high school, Kiyoshi Sakai. Sometimes we would take his older sister and my mother with us. We went all over to places like Kyushu or Hachijo-jima, an island far south of Tokyo.

One day I overheard a customer talking about a *kappo* counter restaurant in Kyoto. For Japanese chefs, Kyoto is a very special place with its own unique food culture and traditions, and the *kappo* counter represents the height of this cuisine, with master chefs preparing seasonal dishes from the freshest ingredients right in front of their customers. The cuisine features varieties of fish that we never use in sushi, such as *hamo* (pike conger) and *okoze* (scorpion fish). The customer described dishes I had never eaten or even seen before, such as *kabura mushi* (grated Japanese turnip steamed with fish), *amadai no sakamushi* (tilefish steamed with sake), clear clam soup, and ginger rice. I decided that I just had to taste these things for myself.

Once again, my friend Sakai accompanied me. In Japan, you can't just walk into a restaurant like this off the street. You need an introduction, so I asked the guest at Matsuei-sushi to make us a reservation. Sakai and I were barely more than twenty, and I'm sure people must have wondered what youngsters like us were doing there. For our part, we came expecting to spend the better part of our scanty wages, and this made us pretty nervous. What would we do if we couldn't pay for it all? Still, nothing could compare to the thrill we experienced when served exotic dishes we'd never seen before. After that, I saved my money and returned many times.

This kind of study could only be done by experiencing the food with my own palate. Although these frequent food-tasting trips required what for me was a huge sum of money, the purpose was not simply to eat good food, but to gain priceless experience. From the local Kyoto cuisine, I learned such valuable lessons as the flavor of Japanese soup stock and how to use tofu, *yuba* (bean curd sheet), seasonal vegetables, and other ingredients that aren't used in sushi. To gain this experience, I had to push the limits of my capacity, but those lessons form the foundation that allows me to make Japanese cuisine other than sushi. Aiming high and paying for it from my own pocket kept me on my toes and motivated me to absorb everything I could.

There are many excellent restaurants all over the world now, and I constantly remind the staff of every Nobu that experience is the best teacher. "Off you go and spend your money," I tell them.

THE SEARCH FOR GOOD FOOD LEADS ME TO MY FUTURE WIFE

Sakai was a very good friend. He joined me in my *kappo* counter trips to Kyoto, even though he was involved in construction, not in the restaurant business. He had always been a top student, whereas I had always been at the bottom of the class. The only certificate I ever received in elementary school was for "good health." And, of course, I had been expelled from high school. Yet for some reason, we got along really well. He was just a great guy.

The Osaka World Expo was held in 1970. Sakai and I decided to go and hopped on a bullet train bound for Osaka. When we saw the hordes of people headed to the same place, however, we got cold feet and decided to carry on past Osaka to Kurashiki in Okayama. There, we dropped in on Shin'ichiro Fujita, the director of the Ohara Museum of Art, who was a frequent guest at Matsuei-sushi. When he saw us, he called up a restaurant named Takoshin.

"There's a young sushi chef visiting from Tokyo," we overheard him say. "Please feed him and his friend as much as they can eat."

Sakai and I looked at each other and whispered, "All right!"

The food at Takoshin was so delicious that we went there for lunch the next day as well. Of course, the second time we paid for our own meal. Even though it was only lunch, it was shockingly expensive, and we felt guilty just thinking about how much Mr. Fujita must have paid for our dinner the night before. That evening we stayed at an inn called Tsurugata, again at Mr. Fujita's introduction. It was there that I met Yoko, the woman who would become my wife. At the time, however, we didn't speak to each other or feel any tug of destiny.

About a year later, Mr. Fujita dropped into Matsuei-sushi when he was visiting Tokyo. With him, he brought Yoko. He had gotten her a job working in the cloakroom of a restaurant in Shiba, Tokyo, and had invited her to come with him. He pointed out to us that we had met the previous year at the inn in Kurashiki, and, although neither of us remembered the other at all, we politely said, "Oh, yes, now that you mention it."

In that era, sushi chefs in Japan were often treated as mavericks, and girls certainly didn't view them as desirable marriage partners. With only two days off a month, I had no time to date a girl anyway. But somehow I felt we were a match. The fact that she was older than me actually made me feel more comfortable.

We began dating and were married the following year. I was just twenty-three, and she was one year older.

TRYING OUT NEW DISHES WHEN THE BOSS WASN'T LOOKING

Around the same time, the senior coworker who I had been working under opened his own restaurant, and I became senior sushi chef at Matsuei-sushi. The boss left most of the work to me, and, although perhaps I shouldn't boast, many of the guests had become my fans.

There were many bars and restaurants in that area of Shinjuku, and Matsuei-sushi's regulars often visited several establishments in a single night. Occasionally, someone might arrive quite drunk after closing and demand a drink. Because I was live-in staff, I would come out right away to let them in and prepare them a snack and a drink. Having watched the way my boss treated his customers, I think I just automatically assumed I should do my best to fulfill their requests, regardless of how unreasonable they might be. They affectionately called me "Matchan" and would stop by casually for a drink and a bite when pub-hopping. Some of those who woke me up after hours are now regular guests at Nobu Tokyo. They were not just my seniors in age but also in experience, and as they were active on the world stage, the tales with which they entertained me greatly influenced my life.

Once my boss began leaving things more up to me, I was no longer satisfied just to make what people ordered. The desire to experiment with new ideas surged inside me. For example, I was one of the first to serve sardine and Pacific saury as sashimi at a time when few chefs served these fish raw. In summer, I purchased fresh sea bass and served it as *arai* (thin slices in ice water) or as *nikogori* (jellied fish) to accompany drinks. Wanting to try my hand at some of the *kappo* dishes I had eaten in Kyoto, I sometimes bought fish without asking my boss for permission. When he happened to find out, he would grumble about my unnecessary expenditures.

THE ORIGIN OF MY PHILOSOPHY "PUT YOUR HEART INTO YOUR WORK AND COOK WITH PASSION"

Of course, whenever I made something new, I would recommend it to whoever was there. Matsuei-sushi guests were all quite wealthy and well established in their fields, and I'm sure that the dishes I was capable of producing would have been nothing new to them. But to me, they were my creations. I really wanted people to try them, and my guests must have sensed my enthusiasm because they all urged me to go ahead and serve what I had made.

I was always trying to imagine how each guest would respond to a new dish. My longing to see delight on their faces seemed to spark one idea after another. All my thoughts were focused on how to make them happy. I planned what to say when recommending a new dish, how to present it and how to explain it. This enthusiasm was infectious, and my guests responded in kind. I think that this was the origin of my philosophy "Put your heart into your work and cook with passion." In particular, I think that this experience of preparing food for my guests while watching their reactions across the counter inspired the very popular Chef's Omakase course at my first restaurant, Matsuhisa.

I was just a simple-hearted sushi chef who loved his work. The customers treated me with good-humored affection, perhaps because they liked my attitude and thought I was an interesting young man. The well-known interior designer Tadashi Akiyama, in particular, taught me many things.

Once, however, I went too far. Keisuke Serizawa, the famous textile designer, was at the counter, and in my eagerness, I kept pressing him to try one new dish after another. "Let me eat what I want!" he finally exclaimed.

Although some customers could be a bit demanding, I never lost my temper. I loved listening to them, and, as I was young, I could listen without bias to anything they had to share. I often asked them questions and soaked up their answers like a sponge. If they said, "Give me another drink," I said, "Yes, sir," and if they said, "You want one, too?" I said, "Yes, sir." Being young has its advantages.

With Mr. Akiyama.

AN OFFER TO START A SUSHI RESTAURANT IN PERU

I think it was right around the time Yoko and I were talking about getting married that Luis Matsufuji began frequenting Matsuei-sushi. A second-generation Japanese-Peruvian, Luis was a prominent businessman whose parents had made it rich growing black pepper in Peru. Probably everyone in the capital of Lima knew his name. He was a dynamic person who went fishing on the Amazon with the well-known Japanese novelist Takeshi Kaiko.

When he came to Matsuei-sushi, he would sit at the counter and tell me stories of Peru. Before I knew it, the picture he painted of the Amazon overlapped with my image of my father in Palau. Because he was so dynamic, I found his stories captivating. Spurred on by my enthusiastic response, he would become even more animated. He became one of my fans, and we hit it off well. One day he said, "You should come to Peru. We'll start up a sushi restaurant together."

Here was a once-in-a-lifetime opportunity to fulfill both of my dreams simultaneously: to be a sushi chef and to work overseas. I knew immediately that that was what I wanted to do. But I owed Matsuei-sushi a lot. My boss had literally been like a father to me. I had even asked him to serve as the *nakodo* (ceremonial matchmaker) at our wedding, a role as important as best man. How could I ask him to let me go to Peru? I agonized over this for some time. When I finally made up my mind and consulted him, he suggested that I go and see what it was like first. And that was how I ended up going alone to Peru to investigate.

It was my first trip overseas ever. But as my image of "going overseas" was not going to New York or London but to "primitive lands" like my father, Peru fit my image perfectly. On my first visit, the country seemed backward. There were only three or four Japanese restaurants in Lima at that time. Having come all this way, I wanted to see what working there might be like and spent a few days working at a restaurant called Tokyo Sushi. Although they told me many things, my skills were frankly superior. Despite the fact that the fish varieties used were unfamiliar, I was confident I could prepare them better.

Yoko and I decided to move to Peru after our wedding. But when my mother heard this, she rushed over to our apartment and, falling to her knees, grabbed my legs and burst into tears. "Please don't go!" she begged. Before World War II, many Japanese had immigrated to Peru, but quite a number of families that had boarded ships bound for South America never returned to Japan. Having heard such stories, my mother must have been worried that she would never see us again. I explained that times had changed. Far from being a frontier land, Peru could now be reached by plane, and we would not be gone for life. In the end, I managed to convince her to let us go.

Once You've Hit Rock Bottom, Impatience Vanishes

—

A series of failures in foreign lands

PERU LIMA MATSUEI-SUSHI OPENS

I felt guilty for leaving Matsuei-sushi after all my boss had done for me, but he gave me a *noren* curtain emblazoned with the words "Peru Lima Matsuei-sushi." He'd had it specially made for the entrance of our new restaurant. I was thrilled. This custom, which is known as *norenwake* in Japanese, showed that he believed me capable enough to use his name.

Many of our friends and relatives came to see us off at Haneda Airport. With the *noren* carefully stowed in our luggage, my wife and I boarded the plane, which took us via Canada to Peru on the opposite side of the world from Japan. It was Yoko's first trip abroad. She spoke some English, but I spoke none, and I had no Spanish, either. Still, I wasn't concerned. After all, this was my second trip to Peru, and, this time, I was traveling with Yoko. It was 1972, and the Japanese economy was booming.

In Peru, we relied on the Matsufuji family. Locally, Luis was known as Don Lucho, and he really was the don of the family. His four younger brothers—Jorge, Dario, Carlos, and Mitsuo— were likewise influential businessmen. A second-generation Japanese-Peruvian cameraman named José Hitotsuishi and his Okinawan-born wife, Natsuko, also took good care of us. When they invited us to their home, Natsuko fed us things like *soki-soba* (Okinawan-style noodles) and a local chicken and rice dish called arroz con pollo.

Peru is where I first encountered cilantro, which Peruvians love. Put off by its pungent smell, I couldn't eat it at first. But because it is an essential part of Peruvian cuisine, I decided to train myself and tried adding it to food in different ways, starting with a single leaf in clear broth. Eventually, I grew to like it. Now, it has become an essential ingredient in several dishes on the Nobu menu. Every region in the world has certain foods that are cherished by the local people. In Peru, I learned the importance of tasting and getting used to unfamiliar foods, instead of deciding that I don't like something before I've even tried it.

Most Japanese-Peruvians are descendants of immigrants who began crossing the sea at the end of the nineteenth century. To me, they seemed to have retained the culture of "good old" Japan. This was reflected in their style of speech and the use of polite expressions, their ethics and respect for others, and their hospitality. They were generous of spirit and strictly disciplined, and a firm inner conviction permeated their words and actions. My grandmother was born during that same period, and because she raised me, I found the atmosphere in the Japanese-Peruvian community very comfortable.

There was another reason I felt comfortable in Peru. Tokyo, where I had lived and worked for many years, was in the midst of rapid economic growth, whereas Lima was still peaceful and quiet, despite being the capital of Peru. It reminded me of my hometown in Saitama where I had spent my childhood.

We renovated a place where Don Lucho had once lived and called it Matsuei-sushi. It could accommodate a total of about one hundred guests, with a twelve-seat sushi bar on the first floor and tables and two private rooms on the second floor. Yoko and I chose to live above the restaurant.

This was my very first time running a restaurant on my own. Although I had complete confidence in making sushi and preparing fish, I would be lying if I said that I wasn't a little anxious about whether we would succeed. Still, I was optimistic that things would turn out all right. The economy in Peru was good, and many major Japanese trading companies had branches there. Our main guests were Japanese businessmen and second-generation Japanese-Peruvians. Thanks to them, the restaurant prospered, and we were kept very busy.

As I couldn't possibly cover the entire restaurant on my own, I invited two friends from Japan, Tsuneo Asakura and Toshi Konishi, to join me. Asakura had worked as a chef at the Japan Airlines Flight Crew Training Center in Napa, California, while Konishi had been the *itamae*, or chef, at Izumi, a restaurant in Shinjuku that served *chazuke*, a bowl of hot rice and condiments with hot green tea or *dashi* poured over the top. I used to visit this restaurant on my days off. Neither of them had made sushi before, so I taught them how. It was great fun working with these Japanese friends every day, and business was good enough that we could enjoy occasional holidays.

My friends and I studied Spanish together during our breaks. I think that I learned the language not just through books or a teacher, but also while moving and working. For example, I'd be in the kitchen on the second floor cooking and would need a bamboo basket from the sushi bar on the first floor. Looking down from upstairs, I could see it, but not knowing the Spanish word, I couldn't ask for it. Feeling a bit frustrated, I would run downstairs, grab it, and say, "What's this?" "*Canasta*," the Peruvian staff would say, and the next time I would be able to call out, "Bring me the *canasta*." That's how I gradually learned Spanish. As I became more fluent, my work became easier. The merchants from whom I always bought fish came to know my preferences and would set some aside for me. One of the women who used to work there now works for Konishi's restaurant in Peru. I was very moved to see her again when I visited in 2012.

GETTING CONGER EEL CHEAP IN PERU

In Lima, it was easy to get excellent ingredients for making sushi, including black porgy, flounder, and octopus. In the early morning, the stalls of the city's largest fish market were lined with fish and shellfish that had been trucked long distances, such as Patagonian toothfish (also known as Chilean sea bass), abalone, and scallops. In the evening, fishermen crowded along a street called Calle Capón in the city center to sell their fresh catch. Prices were never indicated, which meant that everything had to be negotiated. I was careful to buy as cheaply as possible and never reveal what we could actually afford.

One day, I went to Calle Capón and found a conger eel. Excited, I asked the vendor, "Can you get more?"

He looked at me suspiciously. "What do you want that for?" he asked.

Peruvians, I realized, must have no custom of eating conger eel. My bargaining instincts kicked in immediately. In my halting Spanish, I explained. "My dog comes from Japan. He loves eel. But in Peru, no eel. Now he's very homesick."

The vendor grinned. "In that case," he said, "come again tomorrow."

The next day I went again and found a heap of conger eels. The vendor told me that the fishermen caught plenty of them when they set their traps at night. "How much?" I asked.

"Take the whole lot and give them to your dog," he replied. I felt bad taking them for free, so I gave him a bit of money. Needless to say, Matsuei-sushi's special that night was conger eel.

It soon became a popular item on our menu, and a Japanese chef from another restaurant went looking for some at the market. Coming across the vendor who always saved them for me, he asked him how much. "Oh, do you have a Japanese dog, too?" the vendor asked. The truth was out, but Lima was a good-natured place. The next time I met that vendor, he just winked at me and laughed. Peru has since become an exporter of conger eel.

CLASHING WITH MY PARTNER OVER THE COST OF INGREDIENTS

Once the restaurant began to flourish, Yoko and I, with the help of a Japanese businessman, moved into a large mansion of about ten thousand square meters, complete with a maid and gardener. Just before our eldest daughter was born, we invited my mother to come and help with the baby. It was also a chance to reassure her that we were doing fine. This was the woman who had clung to my legs and begged me not to leave Japan,

Matsuei-sushi in Lima, Peru.

but she was so taken with life in Peru that she stayed a total of ten months and only returned to Japan when my eldest brother insisted that it was time she came home. Until she passed away at the age of ninety-three, she kept saying that she wanted to go back to Peru again. Those ten months must have seemed like heaven to her.

This stable life, however, lasted only three years. One night Don Lucho and his family called a meeting. When I got there, they were already drinking. Fortified with liquor, they began saying things that went against my convictions, such as profit comes before quality. When I tried to protest, they cut me off in Spanish. Lucho owned 51 percent of the shares in our business while I owned 49 percent. Laws prevented foreigners from holding a majority stake, and Lucho had more clout than I did, even though the difference was only 2 percent.

I want to use the best ingredients possible. This was true then, and it's still true now. Good-quality ingredients are what makes it possible for chefs to serve their guests with confidence and provide the finest service. So it's only natural for a chef to select the best fish that are available. It's instinct. Good quality inevitably means a higher price. But if instead of trying to squeeze out extra profit, we set a reasonable price that matches the quality of the ingredients, we will inevitably please our guests. Besides, the majority of guests at our restaurant were Japanese businessmen who were accustomed to eating good food all over the world and frequented the best restaurants in Japan. We couldn't get away with cutting corners just because we happened to be a sushi bar in Peru.

If this happened to me now, or if we could have spoken in Japanese, I might have been able to listen better to what they were saying and find a compromise. But I was young, and the fact that they were drunk and yelling at me made me angry. I felt that they didn't understand me and were bossing me around. The blood rushed to my head, and I couldn't be bothered trying to reason with them. Before I realized it, I had blurted out, "I'm quitting, then." I have no memory of Lucho's expression when I told him that. I was probably too upset for it to even register.

I had lost my job and was without a plan, despite having a wife and child to support. Japan was very far away, and I was stuck in Peru, a stranger in a foreign land. My family and I might be turned out into the street at any moment. But I could not turn back, and I did not want to return to Japan. I decided to consult Teruo Nishimura, one of our regulars. Mr. Nishimura happened to be the First Secretary at the Japanese embassy in Peru and had a great sense of humor. Our families had become so close that my mother and his had gone back to Japan together. He introduced me to Mikado, a Japanese restaurant in Argentina where he had once been stationed. We packed our bags, and a few weeks later Yoko and I flew to Buenos Aires with my pots and pans and our one-year-old daughter. Even then, I wasn't worried.

THE FRUSTRATION OF BEING UNABLE TO DO THE WORK I WANT

Mikado was a small restaurant run by the Imamura family. In addition to myself, two Japanese-Argentinians worked there. The salary was a little under $200 a month. Fortunately, prices in Argentina were the lowest in the world, and we were somehow able to make ends meet. We lived in a one-bedroom apartment owned by Mr. Imamura.

But the restaurant had few customers; often we had only one party per day. Argentinians don't eat supper until about nine or ten at night, and customers tend to linger. In addition, Argentina is a land of meat eaters. At that time, a whole beef tenderloin only cost a dollar and fifty cents, which made it far cheaper to eat meat than fish. In such an environment, few people bothered to order sushi, which was expensive, and I only received a few orders a day.

This gave me plenty of free time, and I began to read a lot. It was hard to get Japanese books, so I read whatever I could get my hands on. I remember plowing through all twenty-six volumes of Sohachi Yamaoka's *Tokugawa Ieyasu* and the eight volumes of Ryotaro Shiba's *Saka no Ue no Kumo* (*Clouds Above the Hill*). Buenos Aires was beautiful and a great place for taking walks with our daughter in the park. I also enjoyed fishing in the pond in Palermo Park in the city center. There were ginkgo trees, and we used to gather the nuts in autumn and eat them. Although still in my twenties, I felt like I was living the life of a retiree.

From the outside, it probably looked like a luxurious lifestyle, but I really wanted to work and was quite frustrated at being so underemployed. After over a year of this, Yoko became pregnant with our second child. For the first time since I had moved overseas, I started to feel anxious. I was worried that when our family increased, I might get stuck in this pattern for the rest of my life, and was beginning to question whether I should keep on like this.

Around this time, I learned that the interior designer Tadashi Akiyama, who had taken me under his wing when I worked at Matsuei-sushi in Shinjuku, was coming to Peru to attend the wedding of Don Lucho's younger brother Dario. I begged Yoko to let me use what little cash we had to buy a plane ticket and flew to Peru to meet him. It was he who had introduced me to Don Lucho in the first place, a meeting that had led me to Peru, and I felt that I owed him an explanation. Even more, I wanted to consult him about my future.

When I asked him what I should do, Mr. Akiyama was blunt. "You've already given it your best shot, so it's time to smarten up and go back to Japan. You're a good sushi chef. You might as well be in Japan working rather than wasting time worrying about your future in a foreign country." Thanks to his advice, I decided to go back. We packed our bags immediately, and with my pots and pans, my young daughter, and my pregnant wife, I crossed the Pacific Ocean again, this time in the opposite direction.

REDUCED TO POVERTY IN JAPAN

I had left Japan with a dream, only to return disillusioned. When I got back, I was in for another shock. Having been away four years, I called up everyone I knew and suggested that we get together, but they all made excuses. I'm pretty sure they were afraid I would ask them for money. I felt forsaken and very alone.

We went straight to my family home in Sugito, but it wasn't easy living there with a wife and child. The only person who welcomed me back warmly was my friend Sakai, and so I turned to him for advice. He invited us to move out near him and found us a place in Yono, a city in Saitama Prefecture. He even let our family of three stay with him and his family for a few days until we were moved in.

Our new home was a tiny six-tatami-mat room. Though it was old and dilapidated, we were relieved to finally have our own space where we didn't have to worry about getting in anyone else's way. Our second daughter was born while we lived there. The night Yoko went into labor and was in the delivery room, Sakai and another good friend, Yoshizaki, stayed with me and my daughter in our run-down apartment until morning.

I had to find work on my own. My first job was at a sushi shop in Yono, but I couldn't agree with the owner's approach. Perhaps I didn't like being treated like an errand boy and ordered to "Do this" and "Do that." Anyway, I didn't last very long there. Around that time, a friend from the gang of delinquents I used to hang out with in high school opened a sushi restaurant in Konosu, and asked me to help him. This meant commuting from Yono to Konosu every day. Even so, life in Yono wasn't bad. Though poor, we never had to worry about what anyone else thought, and we were happy just being together as a family and having a roof over our heads. I never missed the luxurious life we had led in Peru. At the same time, however, I felt uneasy because I couldn't see any future for us there. It was as if I could see the dream I had cherished from childhood crumbling before my eyes. Once again, I began to agonize over whether I should go on like this. While my friend who ran the restaurant in Konosu was very good to me, I found it hard to be indebted to him for the work.

Then I heard that a friend of Nobuo Kaneko, an actor well known as a gourmet, was going to start up a restaurant in Alaska and was looking for a partner. Kaneko had been a regular at Matsuei-sushi, and once again Mr. Akiyama arranged for me to meet him. Through Mr. Akiyama's introduction, it was decided that I would go to Alaska. By that point, I didn't care where I went or under what conditions: I just wanted to get away from Japan. I felt ashamed, as if I had failed. It seemed as if almost all my friends had disappeared and everyone had given me the cold shoulder. Going to Alaska was my escape.

FORWARD FROM THE BRINK OF DESPAIR—A MILLIMETER A DAY!

I begged Yoko to give me just one more chance, then set off alone for Anchorage, while she and our two children went to her family home in Kurashiki. I had to borrow the entire sum for my airfare.

The restaurant was still under construction, and, for the next six months or so, I wielded a saw and hammer to help build it. Kioi, a Japanese restaurant, finally opened at the beginning of October, and my family came to join me from Japan. Business was brisk right from the start, and I breathed a sigh of relief. On Thanksgiving, we closed the restaurant and took our first holiday since the opening. My family and I were at the home of Masatoshi Tauchi, a Japanese friend who worked at a different restaurant, when suddenly, the phone rang. It was my partner at Kioi.

"Come quick!" he said. "There's a fire!!"

At first, I thought it was a bad joke, but when I stepped outside and looked in the direction of the restaurant, the sky was crimson, and smoke was rising in the air. Then I heard the fire engines.

Borrowing Tauchi's car, I rushed over. It was late November, and snow was falling on Anchorage. The restaurant burned red against the snow-covered streets. The fire had engulfed the building and was burning so fiercely that I couldn't even get close. The falling snow vaporized in the flames that lit the night sky. I couldn't believe what I saw. The restaurant had only been open fifty days. My mind and my whole body went numb with despair. As I stood there in stunned disbelief, scenes from Shinjuku, Peru, Argentina, and Saitama swirled through my head like the images in a revolving lantern, then evaporated. With each vanishing image, I felt as though my body was being whittled away. Flames and smoke rose before my eyes. The building crackled and roared as it came crashing down . . . *This is it*, I thought. *My life is over.*

I have no idea how I got home that night. When I came to my senses, I was sprawled across the table. I drank some water and threw it right back up. My legs were so weak, I couldn't stand. My brain was empty. Neither my mind nor my body registered anything that was said to me. What was I to do? . . . *Ah . . . Enough . . .* , I thought. *I might as well die . . .*

For a while, all I could think about was death and how to go about dying. Should I get lost in the mountains and just disappear? Should I throw myself into the sea?

This period could have lasted a week or just a single night. I had no sense of time.

It was Yoko who saved me. She never left my side. Later, she told me, "I knew that you could rise above it. I was sure that you would carve a path to our future; that you would make me happy." It was her belief in me that carried me through.

As time passed, my awareness crawled back from the brink of despair and drew closer to reality. The innocent laughter of my children reached my ears. They knew nothing of what was going on and were simply overjoyed to have their father home. Their laughter sounded angelic. At that moment, I thought, *I'll give it another try! This time I'll be patient. I'll keep moving forward one step at a time, even if it's just a millimeter a day.*

Until then, somewhere inside I had always been conscious of the success of my friends, some of whom now rode around in Mercedes-Benzes. Ambitious, I had wanted to be successful, too. But at that moment, I let go of everything. I had hit rock bottom, and there was nowhere further to fall. For the first time in my life I felt totally detached.

My wife is standing by me. My children are alive and well. I may not be feeling great myself, but I've done my best and survived another day. I was ready to accept that this was good enough. For the first time, I could really live each day without feeling driven.

Even now, just remembering what happened in Alaska makes me tremble. But I think that losing so much in my late twenties is what led me to my simple way of life. I work hard to make good food and provide good service, not because I want to own a lot of restaurants or make a lot of money, but because I want to make my guests happy.

GOING SOLO TO LOS ANGELES AND VOWING TO MAKE A COMEBACK

Although the restaurant had burned down, I had come all the way to Alaska, so I thought I would stay and try again. But my partner decided not to sponsor my visa, and I had no energy left to try and negotiate one for myself. I could not stay, yet I did not even have enough money to buy tickets to Japan. That is when our neighbor, Ko Ishizu, stepped in. Ishizu was a pilot with Japan

Airlines and the nephew of Kensuke Ishizu, the founder of VAN Jacket Inc. He provided tickets for all four of us, plus a loan of five hundred dollars. Our friendship continues to this day. Really, I owe him my life.

I happened to know a sushi chef named Mr. Seki in Los Angeles. We had met when I was on my way back from Argentina. When the restaurant in Alaska burned down, I called him to ask for help. "Just get yourself here right away," he said. I made a brief stop in Japan first, though, because I needed to take my family home, and there was the issue of the visa as well.

Coming back was even more miserable than our return from Argentina. When I left for Alaska, I had announced to everyone that this was my last chance, yet here I was, back again. As before, it was Sakai who helped us out. He arranged for everything we needed and, thanks to him, I was able to make sure that Yoko and the children made it to her parents' home in Kurashiki. A week later, I boarded a plane for Los Angeles as if running away yet again. I had one suitcase and a total of twenty-five dollars.

Mr. Seki introduced me to Mitsuwa, a small, newly opened Japanese restaurant owned by Mr. Hiro Nishimura, a respected chef and pioneer of Japanese cooking in Los Angeles who had cooked for Emperor Showa during his visit to the city. Mr. Nishimura ran the restaurant with his family, and I was put in charge of its six-seat sushi bar.

In those days, you could still travel to America without a visa and apply for permanent residency. Mr. Nishimura prepared the application for me and taught me the basics I would need to survive in America, such as how to get a credit card and how to rent an apartment. He also sold me a car at a very low price because it was hard to get around Los Angeles without one.

My English was minimal, but I had picked up some Spanish in Peru and that is what I used in my attempts to communicate with customers at the sushi counter. This actually came in very handy as there are many Spanish speakers in Los Angeles. Word soon got around that the sushi chef at Mitsuwa spoke Spanish, and I gained a following of regulars, many of whom still come to Matsuhisa and Nobu.

MY WIFE'S COURAGE REUNITES OUR FAMILY

Meanwhile Yoko was struggling. She applied to the American embassy in Japan for a visa but was turned down. The embassy could not issue visas to the family of someone who was working illegally in the United States, which was basically what I was doing because I didn't have a visa yet. We stayed in touch mainly through letters.

After living apart for more than half a year, Yoko finally took action. Bringing our two daughters and my pots and pans, she traveled as a visitor to Los Angeles. She was very nervous when going through customs. Later she told me, "The customs officer winked at me. I'm sure he knew he shouldn't be letting me through, but when he saw how determined I was, he must have decided to let me go anyway." She and our two daughters stayed, and two years later our whole family was given permanent residency.

Thanks to Mr. Nishimura of Mitsuwa, who helped us get our green cards, and to the courage of my wife, our family was now able to live together without fear. When we received our green cards, Mr. Nishimura sent me out into the world. "You're free now," he told me. "You could make more money working elsewhere, so go wherever you like." Mr. Nishimura helped me at one of the most difficult times of my life, taught me the skills I needed to live in America, and then willingly let me go, rather than trying to tie me down with feelings of obligation. He was both a very strict and a very generous man.

UNITING COOKING METHODS LEARNED IN SOUTH AMERICA WITH SUSHI

I soon found a job at Osho, a Japanese restaurant chain that had three shops in Los Angeles, and was put in charge of the eight-seat sushi counter. Regulars from Mitsuwa also followed me there. This is when I first began experimenting with original cuisine, drawing on my experience in Peru and Argentina.

Because Lima, Peru, is right on the sea with a good supply of fresh seafood, its residents often eat raw fish. For example, ceviche, a popular local dish, is basically raw fish marinated in lemon juice, and I thought it could be adapted for a sushi restaurant. Traditionally, however, it's marinated for so long that the flesh turns white. Accustomed to the delicious flavor of fresh sashimi, I felt that the lemon overpowered the flavor of the fish, which meant that no matter what kind of fish was used, they all ended up tasting the same. To me, this seemed a waste.

In Japanese cuisine, a bit of *sudachi* juice is often squeezed on the fish slices used to top sushi. Taking a hint from this, to retain its distinctive flavor, I mixed the seafood with the ceviche sauce just before serving instead of marinating it for longer. As restaurants in America didn't serve ceviche back then, this dish provided a taste of home for the many Hispanics who lived in Los Angeles. The lemony fragrance actually brought out the distinctive flavor of the seafood, making it even more delicious. It was soon a popular item on the menu.

Many years later, this dish made its way to Peru where it was also enthusiastically embraced. The government of Peru even appointed me as a tourist ambassador for promoting Peruvian cuisine to the world. I was honored and happy to be able to repay the kindness that so many Peruvians had shown me when I lived there.

One day, at an Italian restaurant, I tried soft shell crab for the first time. Soft shell crabs are eaten whole, either sautéed or fried, just after they've shed the hard outer shell, leaving only a soft shell beneath. They were so good that I wanted to try cooking them myself. I bought some immediately and served them deep-fried. One of my guests, however, remarked, "This is a sushi bar. You should make it into a sushi roll." Though surprised, I followed his advice. It tasted great. That was the origin of Soft Shell Crab Rolls, a Nobu signature dish.

Another signature dish, Black Cod with Miso, also originated around this time. Americans love tender-fleshed fish such as salmon, tuna, and *hamachi* (young yellowtail). Taking a hint from this, I went to the market to search for types of fish that would please them. There I found frozen black cod, which was quite cheap. I was instantly inspired to make *saikyo-yaki*, which involves curing the fish in Kyoto-style white miso overnight and then grilling it. At that time, it was almost impossible to find this kind of miso in the States, so I added *mirin* (sweet cooking wine), sugar, and other ingredients to ordinary white miso and then tried packing the cod in it. In Japan, we usually wrap the fillets of fish in cotton cloth and coat these with miso, but instead I placed the fish directly into the miso mixture. When grilled, it was succulent and tender. Americans are less accustomed to eating high-protein white-fleshed fish, but this one struck them as delicious, and it became another instant hit.

Word soon spread that interesting and innovative cuisine could be had at Osho. The sushi counter was always full, with a long line of people waiting outside.

At the counter of Osho.

COVERT PLANS TO SELL THE RESTAURANT
AND FEAR OF LOSING MY JOB AGAIN

I had pulled myself up from rock bottom, found a job I enjoyed, and was making enough income to gradually pay off my debts. I could even take a few holidays and was very happy living with my family of four in our little apartment. Now that my worries were over, I just wanted to keep pleasing my guests with good sushi and innovative cuisine. About six years after I began working at Osho, however, a customer who worked for a real estate agent told me that the restaurant was up for sale. "Are you going to be okay?" he asked.

That's ridiculous! I thought. But, as the saying goes, where there's smoke, there's fire. I knew that it was a common practice in the States to start up a business and then sell it once it turned a profit. This made me uneasy. One day, while out golfing with the owner, I asked him bluntly, "Have you put the restaurant up for sale?"

He looked surprised for a moment, but then said, "Don't worry. I'm not going to sell it." I breathed a mental sigh of relief.

Several months later, however, someone else told me that the restaurant was up for sale, and this filled me with fear. If the restaurant was sold, I might lose my job again. The trauma of that night in Alaska when I had watched the restaurant go up in flames returned to haunt me. Again, I checked with the owner.

"Well, it's true that I was thinking of putting it up for sale a while ago," he said. "But I decided against it. After all, it would be hard for me to make a living without it."

This did not banish my anxiety, but I didn't want to make trouble. "So I can trust you, then, right?" was all I could say.

Rumors of a pending sale, however, continued to reach my ears. It seemed the owner was not being straight with me. Of course, even if the restaurant was sold, I could have chosen to stay and work under the new owner. But it was quite possible that he or she would decide to switch from Japanese cuisine to Italian or French. Still traumatized by the incident in Alaska, it seemed too great a risk not to know who the new owner would be. If the current owner had told me honestly that he was planning to sell the place, I could have plotted my future course of action, but the rumors were setting off warning bells. Unable to trust him, I told him I would be quitting in six months' time. This gave me some leeway to look for a new job. The restaurant was sold soon after I left.

A PROPOSAL AND A PUSH FROM A BENEFACTOR

Around the time that I decided to quit, I happened to make a trip to Japan. Mr. Ito, a judo expert who had been kind to me in Peru, was dying of cancer and wanted to see me. While there, I also met with Mr. Nishimura, the diplomat who had done so much for me and my family in Peru. He had gone on to serve in several other countries in Latin America and was now stationed back in Japan. As we had been like family ever since that time in Peru, I told him what was happening at Osho.

"If that's the case," he said, "you should start up your own place. I'll lend you the money. You can pay me back when you're ready."

His proposal seemed too good to be true. Until then, I had never thought of opening my own restaurant. After what had happened in Alaska, I lacked the courage to even consider it. Yet this was Mr. Nishimura speaking, someone who knew me very well. He knew all about my struggles in Peru, Argentina, and Alaska, and he knew that I had not lasted long at any job after I returned to Japan. He had been to Osho in Los Angeles quite a few times, so perhaps he had sensed that somewhere deep inside I actually wanted to start my own place. He gave me $70,000, just like that. This was the push I needed.

I returned to Los Angeles and began looking for a place to start my own restaurant. I found the perfect location on La Cienega Boulevard in Beverly Hills. It had been a sushi bar, and I was able to rent it with all the goods and furniture included. This is the restaurant now known as Matsuhisa.

3

A Place Filled with the Laughter of My Guests

—

Launching Matsuhisa, my first restaurant

JUST HAPPY TO DO THE WORK I LOVE

The building I found was located on Restaurant Row, a stretch of La Cienega Boulevard known for its stiff competition, with places like Rocky Aoki's Benihana of Tokyo and Lawry's The Prime Rib. It was a bright and glamorous district, and the broad boulevard always bustled with traffic. The place I rented was just an unremarkable one-story building, but all the furnishings were there, and I reopened it as Sushi Bar Matsuhisa. Including the counter, it sat only thirty-eight people. As I recall, there was a Middle Eastern restaurant next door.

Although I rented it with the furnishings intact, I still put a lot of effort into redecorating it. One of my customers from Mitsuwa was an interior designer. Her boyfriend, who was an artist, volunteered to paint the walls and ceiling for free.

"I want a lively restaurant always full of people," I told him.

"All right," he said. "Stand against that wall and pose as if you were filleting a fish." I took my knife and did as he said. He shone a spotlight on me so that my silhouette stood out against the white wall. Then he carefully traced my shadow and painted it in. At that moment, our logo was born. Coupled with the word "Nobu," it has become our symbol. My dream is that this silhouette alone will become so well recognized that it's synonymous with Nobu, just like the Nike swoosh or the Macintosh apple.

The artist also decorated the walls with silhouettes of my regular guests from Osho. Thanks to this, it seems like Matsuhisa is always full of people, which I find very reassuring.

Joe Frieda, who was also a regular guest from Osho, created a little flyer for me on his computer with English descriptions of the menu items. It was very simple, with text only, but it explained such terms as *hamachi no kamayaki* (grilled yellowtail collar) or *horenso no ohitashi* (boiled spinach salad). This was a great help, as it meant that Americans who weren't familiar with Japanese cuisine could understand what I had made for them.

Matsuhisa opened on January 7, 1987. We got off to a good

My silhouette at the sushi bar, which is the basis for the Nobu logo.

start. Although it was a rainy day, the restaurant was full, and many regulars from both Mitsuwa and Osho brought their friends.

It was a huge relief to finally be able to throw myself into the work I loved without holding back out of deference to others. It never occurred to me to think about how much profit I wanted to make. I was just overjoyed to be able to do the work I liked best.

I was thirty-eight. In retrospect, I can see that my feet were not yet firmly on the ground. Still, I was optimistic that as long as I had my knife, things would work out. As the Japanese say, "No matter where you go, food and heaven will follow." Having sunk to the lowest possible depths, I no longer felt anxious or impatient. I was quite content to be moving forward, even if it was just a millimeter a day. Thanks to this attitude, I no longer felt any pressure. For me, it was enough to know that, if I wanted, I could even use the cucumbers growing in the planter at our house to make *kappa maki* (cucumber rolls) for Matsuhisa guests. Being able to make decisions even about such little things made me very happy.

ONE OR TWO HOURS OF SLEEP A NIGHT, EVERY DAY A BATTLE

The restaurant had only just opened, and we had yet to build up trust in our business. As a rule, this meant that I had to pay cash for all my purchases, whether fish or vegetables. No matter how busy I was, I went every morning to the market to choose the ingredients myself. As the vegetable market closed by six in the morning, I went there first to buy produce and packed it in the truck. Next, I would go to a shop called Kawahara to buy fish because I didn't have the connections to buy at the big fish market. I returned to the restaurant by nine in the morning and began prepping food with the young staff.

Our lunch service started at 11:45 a.m. Most restaurants opened at 11:30, but for me those fifteen minutes between 11:30 and 11:45 were priceless. As I did almost everything myself, from making the sushi rice to arranging the fish in the case, there just wasn't quite enough time between 9:00, when I first arrived at the restaurant, and 11:30. Those final fifteen minutes before opening every day were the last spurt, a time during which I was intensely focused.

We closed from around 2:30 until about 5:00 p.m., during which time we got ready for the evening, cooking rolled omelets and grilling conger eel. We opened again at 5:45. I manned the sushi counter with two young sushi chefs, and we had one kitchen staff and two servers. The restaurant's small size allowed us to see our guests' reactions from the sushi counter, and we took advantage of this to offer *omakase*-style service. I was mainly responsible for making sushi, but I also used the kitchen to produce some of the more complex dishes. I stayed focused the entire time the restaurant was open. We had not yet hired anyone to wash dishes, so we cleaned up together and then all six of us went out to eat. By the time we finished, it was two or three in the morning. But

I still had to get up early enough to make it to the market first thing, which gave me only one or two hours of sleep a night. The days seemed to fly by. Compared to the times I had to uproot in South America or the time I lost the restaurant in Alaska, life was more secure and stable, and I now had some peace of mind. While each day seemed like a battle, I didn't mind at all.

FOR MY GUESTS, I CAN DO ANYTHING!

I had learned Spanish in Peru, and after coming to Los Angeles, I learned some English as well. I started off by asking each guest, "Is there anything you can't eat, or anything that you don't like?" I continued conversing with them as they ate, all the while watching their reactions to decide what to make next from the ingredients I had on hand. I no longer had to worry about what someone else would say if I decided to make something that wasn't on the menu. I could do whatever I liked for my guests.

It was through this process of improvising dishes for each individual that the Chef's Omakase developed, and it's now a standard feature at Matsuhisa. I usually prepared a total of about fourteen or fifteen dishes for this course so that the guest could enjoy a broad selection, eating a little at a time. Most restaurants in America served large portions, plunking down two or three plates, and that was it. The Matsuhisa style appeared new and exciting, and word soon got around. Cooking for my guests was even more fun, and I began experimenting with presentation as well.

I didn't set out to do things differently from everyone else. I just wanted to give my guests a taste of all the different ingredients I had bought fresh at the market that day. Serving them one small portion at a time was the natural result. For my guests, however, this was the greatest attraction. On the American restaurant scene, people generally ordered from a course menu. To have a chef create new dishes specifically for each individual provided extra satisfaction. If something wasn't on the menu, it didn't matter. A Japanese visitor might order *yudofu* (lightly boiled tofu), for example, and I would say, "Of course!" I viewed my guests' requests as my homework, exercises that helped me to evolve as a chef. And if the result pleased them, it made me very happy.

NEW DISHES BORN FROM MY PASSION FOR SHARING THE DELICIOUS FLAVORS OF SEAFOOD

Once, when I served an American woman a dish of thinly sliced, white-fleshed sashimi, she told me, "I don't eat raw fish." She didn't even touch it with her chopsticks. I was very disappointed, as I had worked hard to present it attractively. I carried the dish into the kitchen wondering how I could at least get her to try it. Just then, I saw some olive oil heating in a frying pan, almost at the smoke point, and inspiration hit me. I sprinkled some ponzu sauce on the elegantly arranged sashimi and then drizzled the hot olive oil on top. With a sizzling sound, the flesh of the fish turned slightly opaque. Just the surface had been cooked.

I took the dish back to her table. She probably thought I was pretty strange for bringing back food she had already rejected. I knew that she might even be angry with me, but I told her that I had blanched it with hot olive oil and urged her to just try a little bite. Thankfully, she was willing to give it a try. Gingerly, she picked up a slice with her chopsticks and ate it. Then she tried another. And another, until she had finished the whole plate, exclaiming repeatedly, "This is delicious!" She had learned that raw fish doesn't taste fishy. I love this curiosity and open-mindedness that is so typical of Americans.

That is how the Nobu signature dish New Style Sashimi came into being.

After asking a guest if there is anything he or she doesn't like, most chefs would refrain from serving those foods. But as long as there are no allergies, it's possible that our guests can learn to like them if they're given a chance. Take, for example, Tim Zagat, cofounder of the Zagat Survey, which publishes restaurant guides. He didn't like sea urchin. In fact, many Americans are put off by its appearance and texture. But I really wanted him to try it because I could get superbly fresh sea urchin from nearby Santa Barbara. I wrapped some in a *shiso* leaf and nori, dipped it lightly in batter, deep fried it, and served it as tempura with lemon, salt, and pepper. Frying makes sea urchin light and fluffy, so basically I was changing its conventional image. Tim ate six or seven of these that night.

The time a boy who hated seafood of any kind came to Matsuhisa, I really had to think hard. When I asked him what he liked, he said, "Pasta." But as this was a Japanese restaurant, I wasn't about to serve that. Instead, I hit upon the idea of cutting squid into the shape of pasta shells and sautéing them. This inspiration actually came from Yoko, who suggested that sautéed squid might have the same texture as pasta. Fried with asparagus and shiitake mushrooms, the squid shells looked and tasted like pasta to my little guest. He gobbled them up. When he had finished, I told him what it was, and from then on, he was able to eat squid. Called Squid Pasta, this dish is still on our menu.

Wasabi pepper sauce was also invented around this time. The idea came from observing that Americans liked to make a sludge out of wasabi and soy sauce and dip their sashimi in it. From a Japanese perspective, this is not "proper," but when viewed from a different angle, it was clear that this was something Americans liked. I decided to combine the things they liked and make a sauce. I put some powdered wasabi, *dashi* (Japanese soup stock), and soy sauce together in a pan and brought them to a boil, then simmered the mixture until it made a thick sauce. To this, I added some garlic, olive oil or melted butter, and black pepper. When I served it over such things as grilled tuna, scallops, or chicken, it was a huge hit. No bread is served at Matsuhisa because it's a Japanese restaurant, but some of my guests liked this sauce so much that they brought their own bread to dip in it. I bottled it and sold it in the restaurant, and it's now one of our signature sauces and remains popular in Nobu restaurants worldwide.

CUISINE IS LIKE FASHION, ALWAYS EVOLVING

Sometimes when I serve a newly invented dish, it's clear from my customer's expression that he or she isn't 100 percent satisfied, despite insisting that it's delicious. When that happens, I consider what I could do instead. I run it through my mind over and over until I find an answer and come up with another new dish. If I feel that it has really satisfied them, then I'm satisfied, too.

Of course, I can't please everyone, but I believe in testing my own limits to satisfy my guests. You could almost say that it's my guests who create the food I make. I enjoy thinking of all the different possibilities as I try to produce something they will like. In this way, ideas for unique dishes come quite naturally. The new dishes become popular and attract more people. I have simply devoted myself single-mindedly to this process.

Another key element in my approach is giving supporting actors a leading role. If you think of cuisine as a movie, then the stars would be such ingredients as fish and meat. Things like asparagus, watercress, and mushrooms are always relegated to supporting roles. I often think about how I can give ingredients that are usually just an accent for meat a more central part. This is how I come up with menu items that turn sides into mains, such as *shimeji* mushroom tempura and fresh watercress salad, which is watercress leaves dressed with a sauce made from the watercress stems.

Even when I have complete confidence in a dish, if it doesn't take off, I remove it from the menu immediately. On the other hand, those that everyone finds delicious remain on the menu indefinitely. And some dishes that fail to become a hit due to bad timing may catch on when revived a few years later. In this way, my repertoire is constantly being renewed.

Cooking is like fashion in that it reflects the times, just like trends in clothing styles. And just as a fashion designer will introduce new materials and techniques to create new designs, chefs are trailblazers who discover new ingredients and create new dishes, offering new value to their customers through food. Ingredients and cooking techniques are constantly evolving.

HOT FOOD SHOULD BE EATEN HOT, COLD FOOD, COLD

Chefs put their heart and soul into making a meal for their guests. Aware of the spirit in which it is made, the guests savor each dish, and consequently, the food tastes delicious. That, I think, is the nature of a true restaurant.

Put your heart into your work. This is what I repeatedly told my staff when we started out, and what I continue to say now. Guests can always tell whether or not we've prepared their meal with heart and soul. Food that has been made from the heart will touch the hearts of those who eat it.

Have you ever noticed that when you are at the counter and a chef places a freshly made piece of sushi in front of you, there is an instant when the topping settles onto the rice? Properly blended sushi rice has just the right amount of air mixed in. The instant the sushi is placed on your plate, a bit of that air escapes. That's the perfect moment to eat it, and discerning guests don't miss it. This spirit is the true appeal of a sushi-style restaurant. The most crucial element for eating sushi is timing, not any rules about which kind to eat first or how to hold it properly.

Each piece of sushi represents a concentration of infinite details, from the amount of water used to boil the rice to the temperature of the rice when it is shaped in the hand, the amount of pressure exerted, and the size of each topping. The chef pours his heart into making a piece of sushi and places it before a guest who knows what that means. The timing of this give-and-take is the real thrill of a sushi-style restaurant, and it forms the bedrock of all my cooking, not just sushi.

When someone serves me food, I eat it immediately. I want to eat it when it's at the height of perfection out of respect for the spirit of the person who made it. Hot food should be eaten while still hot, chilled food, while still cold. I always tell the servers to move quickly and do the right thing. When they aren't able to serve the food as soon as it's ready, they call out to each other. If no one is free, I will serve the guest myself. I want my guests to eat what I've prepared when it's at its very best.

SUSHI BAR *OMAKASE* IS THE ORIGIN OF NOBU STYLE

I always kept my eyes on my guests, watching their responses while I cooked, served, and explained each dish. I not only explained the ingredients and cooking method, but also what inspired me to make it and the best way to eat it. Because I wanted them to like it. Direct interaction with my guests is still my style. Through this, I learn many things. When something I make is good, my guests praise me. When it's only satisfactory, I can sense it from their expression. If they're not happy with a dish, they often say so quite clearly, and if I listen carefully and make immediate changes, I can still ensure that they leave satisfied.

It's wrong to see an unhappy guest and do nothing until they tell you outright. The only way to ensure that our guests go home happy is to notice when something isn't right before they tell us and to act on it immediately.

When I first apprenticed at Matsuei-sushi, I noticed that the customers never ordered anything from my boss. Without them saying a word, he could make sushi and small bites that perfectly suited their tastes. In the beginning, this was a mystery, but later I realized that this skill is the mark of a professional. I longed to become like him, to be able to serve my guests exactly what they wanted without them saying a word. This, I believe, is the origin of my approach. To provide this kind of service, the chef must constantly observe the expression on each guest's face. That is why every one of my restaurants throughout the world has a sushi counter with a kitchen connected to it.

MY GUESTS' LAUGHTER IS THE BEST BACKGROUND MUSIC

I wanted my guests to feel relaxed, enjoy their food, and fill Matsuhisa with their laughter. For this reason, I deliberately didn't use any background music. For me, the laughter of my guests was the best BGM.

Matsuhisa was small, and therefore it was always buzzing with noise. In addition to talking with the guests at the counter, I also greeted the guests at the tables, served their food, and explained the content. In this way, we became friends. I really enjoyed explaining to them such things as how to eat edamame.

When I first started, it was very unusual for the chef to come out of the kitchen and talk to his clientele. But there was one chef in America who was doing this. His name was Wolfgang Puck, and he launched a new genre of cooking that came to be known as California cuisine. He was the same age as me. He would come out of the kitchen and walk among the tables to speak directly with his guests, explain the food, and joke with them. His restaurant was near Hollywood, too, and was well loved by celebrities. I'm sure that many people came just because they wanted to see him.

Puck has been a major influence on me, even though my field is Japanese cuisine. His approach gave me the courage to apply in Los Angeles what we did at Matsuei-sushi in Shinjuku. We're still good friends and do things like joint charity events together. Now there are guests who come to Matsuhisa specifically to see me. When one of these regulars calls to make a reservation, the receptionist tells them, "Nobu will be here then." That person will then pass on the word to others, and soon that day is totally booked.

THE KEY TO GOOD SERVICE IS TO ANTICIPATE YOUR GUESTS' NEEDS

I think a sushi restaurant needs an element of entertainment. A good sushi chef requires not just superior sushi making skills, but also attentiveness and the ability to make customers comfortable. Conversing with the chef is one of the attractions of a sushi counter.

I don't just make sushi. I talk with the guest in front of me and imagine what I might want if I were him or her. I also think about the best timing to serve each dish. Pacing is important. When I see signs that a guest is wondering what to order next, I might say to them, "If you liked that, you might enjoy this top-

Around the time that Matsuhisa became popular, chairs were placed outside for people waiting in line.

ping that we have in today. Would you like to try it?" That's the kind of attentiveness demanded of a sushi chef and the mark of a professional.

It was Mr. Akiyama who taught me true consideration for others. I was still an apprentice at Matsuei-sushi, and he not only came to our restaurant, but also took me many places on my days off. Knowing that I had no money, he treated me to many different dishes so that I could gain experience. He was knowledgeable not only about his own field of interior design, but also about paintings and antiques, and he willingly explained whenever I asked him a question. Despite being a prominent and highly successful designer, he went out of his way to please a lowly apprentice like me. This thoughtfulness made me very happy.

I observed Mr. Akiyama's behavior from close quarters. When getting on an elevator, he quite naturally allowed women to go first. If someone's glass was empty, he would fill it. When sashimi was served, he would pour soy sauce into each person's dish, not just his own. He always paid attention to what went on around him and would be the first to do something for another person. He seemed to have a sense of what would make others happy. Because I longed to be like him, I think that his behavior rubbed off on me without me even realizing it.

Matsuhisa is the result of my own pursuit of the thought, *What would I want if I were this person?* Some of my guests who have been to Nobu New York or Nobu London tell me that

Matsuhisa is still the best. There's a sense of coming home that they don't experience anywhere else.

This is true for me, too. Whenever I return to Matsuhisa, I feel a sense of relief that I don't feel at any Nobu restaurant. I raised Matsuhisa up from zero, including the menu, the approach to service, and the staff. It looks almost the same as when it first opened, and I have complete confidence in the flavor of every sauce and dressing. Although Nobu may have spread around the world, Matsuhisa will always be my starting point. My roots are Matsuhisa, and because it exists, I can always stay on track.

A TUNA BOUGHT ON IMPULSE INSPIRES NEW SIGNATURE DISHES

As the sole owner of Matsuhisa, I'm free to stock it with whatever I like. When I see something really good, I can almost hear it say, "Please! Buy me," and I can't resist. That's my nature.

One day at the fish market, a tuna stared me straight in the eye. It seemed to be begging me to buy it. Paying no attention to the price, I made it mine. But if the whole tuna was made into sushi, it would have fed several hundred people. And even then, I still couldn't have used it all for sashimi or sushi. I had to think of some other ways. Wondering what would happen if I grilled it, I took a piece of *toro* and cooked it like a steak. Guests who tried it were amazed by the rich, buttery flavor and exclaimed that it was like wagyu beef. This was the birth of the Toro Steak. Although this dish is quite common now, at that time it was totally unorthodox.

My impulse purchase was also the inspiration for Sashimi Salad. Americans are quite health-conscious, and often have salad for lunch. I added some slices of seared tuna to a salad, drizzled it with soy sauce–based dressing, and called it Sashimi Salad with Matsuhisa Dressing. It was a great hit. Because sashimi is raw fish, many Americans felt a little wary of trying it. Adding the words "salad" and "dressing" made the dish sound more familiar. The Matsuhisa dressing I developed for this dish is now used at all Nobu restaurants worldwide.

That tuna cost me a fair bit, but because I went ahead and bought it without worrying about the price, several signature Nobu dishes were born. I definitely made my money back. The way that tuna urged me to buy it reminds me of the dog in the Japanese folktale "Hanasaka Jiisan" that barked at his master to make him dig. Thanks to his dog, the master struck gold.

IMPORTING RAW FISH FROM JAPAN

If you buy the best ingredients and cook them properly, your guests will always be satisfied. Because I loved to see my guests happy, I bought the best ingredients without begrudging the price. No longer content to serve just the kinds of fish available in America,

I began importing fish directly from Japan with the cooperation of Minoru Yokoshima of International Marine Products.

I had another reason for doing this. I wanted to teach the young chefs assisting me at the sushi counter the skills common to sushi bars in Japan. Japanese customers who came to Matsuhisa would often ask the chefs where they learned to make sushi. They would reply rather reluctantly, "In Los Angeles." I felt sorry for them. Because I had learned how to make sushi in Japan, I knew how to dress many different kinds of fish. I wanted to teach them the skills I had learned in the land of sushi by using fish procured there. Then my staff could say with pride that they had learned at Matsuhisa.

As the Japanese saying goes, however, the child does not know the mind of the parent. One day I found a *sayori* (needlefish) in the garbage. A very thin fish, it's hard to fillet and also has a short shelf life. It looked like someone had attempted but failed to fillet it properly and had thrown it away. I reprimanded the chefs quite harshly. "I had this imported for you especially from Japan. Why did you throw it away?! You could at least have thought up ways to cook it!"

To be honest, it's much easier to be a sushi chef on one's own. But I think you can only be considered a full-fledged chef once you can pass on the skills you've learned from others to up-and-coming chefs. Only when an apprentice finally reaches your level can you call yourself a master. Once I had taught them how, my employees could fillet *kohada* (gizzard shad), prepare conger eel, and do many other tasks. This, in turn, took some of the load off me and let me focus on the work I needed to do.

Alone, I could only do the work of one person, but with three or four others, I found that together we could do the work of five or six. It was at this point that I realized the importance of training. It takes time to teach others. If we only consider the work we need to do that particular day, it would be far faster to do it ourselves. But if we don't teach others and cultivate their skills, we'll never have time to do the work we really want to do. This is another of the lessons I learned during this period through repeated trial and error. Many of those I trained now run their own sushi restaurants.

LABOR COSTS ARE CHEAP IF YOU EMPLOY PEOPLE WHO ARE MOTIVATED

As Matsuhisa became increasingly popular, young chefs began coming to us looking for work. If they were highly motivated, I wanted to hire them even if we already had enough staff. Of course, from the perspective of labor costs, this was a waste.

Chefs from other restaurants would give me tips about the people I was interviewing, saying that so-and-so wouldn't last or was a bad character or even telling me that I would be better off not hiring someone. But I felt it was unfair not to give people a second chance because I, too, had failed many times. If they were applying to Matsuhisa because they wanted to start over or learn from scratch under me, then I wanted to give them a chance. After all, I had been given so many chances myself.

Those who were motivated learned quickly and soon became effective members of our team. As a result, our customer volume increased. That alone made it a worthwhile investment. And that was not all. Being surrounded by motivated young people sparked my competitive spirit. Not wanting to be beaten at my own game, I developed a friendly rivalry with my apprentices. Sometimes I vied with the younger chefs to see who could please the guests most with our *omakase* dinner. This increased the energy and vibrancy of the restaurant, attracting even more customers.

Matsuhisa took up half the building. The restaurant that occupied the other half failed to catch on, and the space frequently changed hands. We always had such a long line outside that one of my guests suggested that I might as well rent the whole building. But I didn't even consider this idea. While the extra space would mean that we could accommodate and please even more guests, for me, the thirty-eight-seat Matsuhisa seemed perfect. I did not have any ambition to expand it into a larger restaurant. In the end, however, the building's owner came to me himself and asked me to rent the rest of the space, and, in 1990, that's what I did.

GOOD INGREDIENTS COME FIRST, PROFIT, LATER

I left all the accounting up to my wife. She handled everything, including paying for the ingredients, the rent, and the wages, and managing the restaurant's profits. Thanks to her, I could focus solely on cooking. Without worrying about profit and loss, I could devote myself to my work just for the sake of seeing the delight on my guests' faces. Looking back on it, I realize that this was a very good thing. If I had been balancing the books while doing the cooking, I might never have come up with some of my bolder, more daring dishes. Yoko still tells me, "You had it easy. You got to see the smiles on your guests' faces. It was really hard trying to pay the bills, you know."

In Peru, Argentina, and Alaska, Yoko had never uttered a word of complaint. But not long after Matsuhisa opened, she told me, "At this rate, we won't be able to save any money." This was just around the time that I began importing fish from Japan. Business was booming, but the high cost of ingredients meant that there was nothing left after paying the monthly bills. In fact, for about two years, we made no profit at all, even though the restaurant was always full.

Still, I told her, "We're able to pay all the bills. We're even paying back our loans little by little. Isn't that enough? Please don't say things like that again." That was the last time she ever said anything to me about purchasing for the restaurant.

When a guest sits down at a sushi counter, he or she will ask,

"What have you got today?" As an artisan, the sushi chef takes pride in giving them something that so exceeds their expectations, it surprises them. That is why I gave priority to satisfying my guests before sales or profits. As a result, these guests couldn't wait to tell their friends. "The other night," they would say, "I ate this amazing dish at a place called Matsuhisa." The number of guests continued to increase, and we became known for delivering more than expected. Many of our regulars would ask, "Do you have anything new today?" And I took pleasure in confidently recommending what we had in stock. That is how Matsuhisa came to flourish.

Because I bought good ingredients, I wanted to use them up without wasting anything. Thinking about how to do this inspired new ideas, such as a tartar sauce made by chopping up fish parts not used in sashimi or sushi. The repetition of this process has led to the birth of many new dishes. I wasn't trying to get attention for being original. It was just a natural consequence of experimenting with ways to use up every last scrap and prevent waste.

Much later I talked with Yoko about this. "It's because I didn't have to cut costs for ingredients that we could achieve so much," I said, and I know she understood. I think putting our guests' satisfaction first is crucial. As long as we do that, results will always follow.

LEARNING THE IMPORTANCE OF PRAISE

I think that by coming to America I finally grew up. During my apprenticeship in Japan, I was rapped with the dull edge of a knife if I made a mistake, and the senior staff were sometimes quite mean to me. I learned many things in Peru, Argentina, and Alaska, but I suffered some severe setbacks, too. After I went to Los Angeles, however, things changed. The difference was that everyone praised me.

Americans are good at praising people. When I served them good food, they'd exclaim, "This is fabulous!" and "You're a genius!" It was a bit over the top, yet I couldn't help but get caught up in the spirit of it. *Hear that?* I would say to myself. *You're a genius!* Although I felt slightly embarrassed, I didn't mind at all. In fact, it made me want to try even harder. America is where I learned how important praise is for motivating people to improve.

In Japan, there is a strong tendency to point out people's faults. The Japanese even have a saying: "The nail that sticks out gets hammered down." If I had stayed in Japan and been faced with constant criticism as I tried to create new dishes, I might have given up before even coming close to where I am now and decided to just cook the things I was taught. The world of Japanese craftsmen, including sushi chefs, is generally governed by a strict hierarchy of relationships, but personally I do much better when someone quietly helps me to recognize my mistakes instead of harping on them. While I was working at Matsuei-sushi in Shinjuku, a younger guy from my hometown also began working there. I could have bossed him around, just as the older staff had done to me, but I found it far more enjoyable to be friendly with him than to give him a hard time.

Besides, I had the example of Mr. Akiyama, to whom I owe so much. One of our best guests, he never treated young people with contempt and was kind enough to respond to all my questions. The owner of Matsuei-sushi, too, was a mature man who willingly taught me whatever I asked. Overseas, I saw training approaches that worked fine even though they differed from the system in Japan. Although when I was young I sometimes yelled at the junior staff, my experience overseas taught me that there is no need to do so.

Speaking of being good at praising, my wife, Yoko, is, too. Although I put her through a lot of hardship, she always supported me without complaint. When we talk about those difficulties now, it's clear that she believed I would overcome them all. It's thanks to her, too, that I was able to keep doing my best.

MEDIA ATTENTION ATTRACTS CELEBRITIES

About half a year after Matsuhisa opened, it was featured in the *Los Angeles Times* and *LA Weekly*, and the number of guests doubled. We were all overjoyed to see the restaurant covered in these

With my wife, Yoko, at the opening party of Nobu San Diego.
(Photo by Steven Freeman)

newspapers. The first time it happened, I went out and bought ten copies. The restaurant became so popular it was hard to get a reservation. Although we were run off our feet, for me every day was so much fun that I couldn't get enough.

Two years later I was chosen by *Food & Wine* magazine as one of America's ten best new chefs, and in 1993, the *New York Times* selected Matsuhisa as one of the top ten restaurant destinations in the world. The only restaurant chosen from Japan was Kitcho in Kyoto. This pleased me greatly because, compared to Matsuhisa, which had only opened a few years earlier, Kitcho had a very long tradition.

Shortly after that, we received a reservation for two from someone who had seen us in the *New York Times*. On the day they were scheduled to come, a limousine pulled up in front of Matsuhisa, and out stepped a man in a tuxedo and a woman in a formal evening gown. There are only about fifteen centimeters between the tables in Matsuhisa, and at the time, the tablecloths were covered in plastic. The couple gazed at them perplexed, no doubt wondering if they had come to the right place. I greeted them and asked my usual questions about whether there was anything they didn't like. Then I began serving them the Chef's Omakase, making dishes based on my observations of their reactions. I still remember how happy they looked when they left.

A writer who produced a widely read newsletter happened to become one of our regulars. Thanks to our location in Hollywood, when he wrote us up, many movie stars and celebrities began coming. Even Tom Cruise called to make a reservation, but I had to say no because we were full. Matsuhisa was small, seating only thirty-eight people, so if the counter and tables were already reserved by others, I had no choice but to turn down requests for new reservations, even from an up-and-coming Hollywood star. Later, I got a call from Mike Ovitz, an influential Hollywood agent who was already a familiar face at Matsuhisa. "You shouldn't turn down Tom Cruise," he scolded me. Tom Cruise came on another day and, when I apologized to him in person, he gave me a friendly greeting.

Madonna has been a regular guest from the very beginning. I have known her to stand in line for thirty minutes waiting for a seat when she doesn't have a reservation. She even wrote a comment for the jacket of my first recipe book, *Nobu: The Cookbook*. She also drops into Nobu Tokyo when she's touring Japan.

The day that Barbra Streisand first visited Matsuhisa, one of my guests pointed her out to me. "Nobu," he said, "there's Barbra Streisand. You should go over and greet that table." I did as I was told, but I hadn't a clue who she was. She and her friend were so involved in conversation that I didn't want to interrupt. Returning to the counter, I asked the guest, "So which one is Barbra Streisand?" He burst out laughing.

During the Academy Awards, actors and actresses from around the world come to eat at Matsuhisa. Italian comic actor Roberto Benigni came a few days before the ceremony the year he was nominated for the film *Life Is Beautiful*. I told him, half joking, "If you come here every day, you'll be sure to win." He actually did come every day with his wife, Nicoletta Braschi. On the day of the awards ceremony, I watched it on television, hoping he would win. Benigni leaped onto his chair and raised his arms high when they announced that he had won. I was overjoyed, too. A poster for *Life Is Beautiful* signed by Benigni still hangs on the wall of Matsuhisa.

Although restaurant reviews in newspapers and magazines contributed to Matsuhisa's popularity, I found that they also had a scary side. People who read about Matsuhisa came with high expectations. Knowing that I had to exceed those expectations to satisfy them kept me on my toes. I poured my passion into serving them and drilled into everyone my motto: "Good food, good service, teamwork." Later I learned that chefs from famous restaurants had also come to eat at Matsuhisa.

Major Hollywood producers often used Matsuhisa as a meeting spot for power lunches. I never gave them prima donna treatment, and I think that made them feel relaxed. I treated every guest the same, whether or not they happened to be a celebrity, a major producer, or a critic. Or perhaps it would be more accurate to say that I was so focused on my work, I really didn't have time to pay attention to who was a celebrity and who wasn't. I didn't even recognize Robert De Niro the first time we met, although we were destined to become business partners.

4

Robert De Niro, the Man Who Waited Four Years

—

The beginning of the Nobu management team

MEETING ROBERT DE NIRO

The first time Robert De Niro came to Matsuhisa was in 1988. Roland Joffé, director of *The Killing Fields*, brought him. Although the name Robert De Niro seemed familiar, I had no idea who he was. I hadn't watched any Hollywood movies since going to South America. As Joffé was a regular, I simply prepared food for him and his guest as usual.

De Niro particularly liked the Black Cod with Miso and the Japanese sake Hokusetsu. After the meal, he invited me to join them for a drink. That was our first conversation. Although he lived in New York, he continued to drop by Matsuhisa whenever he was in Los Angeles. Sometimes he came with friends or his agent, and other times with his family. He has a special aura, and the restaurant buzzed with excitement when he was there, yet he always dropped in casually without a bodyguard.

I think it was in 1989 that De Niro first suggested we start a restaurant together in New York. Matushisa had only opened two years earlier, and I was really busy. I couldn't imagine setting up another restaurant somewhere else. But De Niro insisted that I should at least come to New York and see, and his enthusiasm convinced me to go. I stayed at the hotel in the World Trade Center and spent three or four days with him. He invited me to his home, showed me around his office, and took me to see the property he had just bought in Manhattan's Tribeca neighborhood. At the time, Tribeca was a run-down warehouse district. De Niro's building was old. Water dripped from broken pipes, and rats scurried inside. Against this backdrop, he shared with me his vision. "I want to start up a business here. This will be the restaurant space. I'll have a screening room there and my office over here . . ."

My English, however, was too poor for us to carry on any kind of discussion. Although I could follow much of what he said, I couldn't really converse. I listened to his ideas and then, in broken English, tried to explain that I couldn't start another restaurant now because the one in Los Angeles was not quite on its feet. Matsuhisa's popularity was growing, and I could feel the potential for our clientele to keep expanding. But I knew that my staff didn't have enough training yet. Although De Niro's proposal was very attractive, I felt that I should build a solid foundation for Matsuhisa first.

De Niro continued to drop into Matsuhisa, and I continued to treat him like a regular guest, serving him Black Cod with Miso and suggesting newly invented dishes that I thought he might enjoy. When he came, he never mentioned his proposal for a joint venture in New York. In fact, he teamed up with restaurateur Drew Nieporent and turned the property he had shown me into the Tribeca Grill, a restaurant serving American fare, which opened in 1990.

HE WAITED FOUR WHOLE YEARS

Four years after I had turned down his offer, De Niro called me at home. "So, Nobu, how about it?" he said. "Why don't you come to New York again?"

At first, I wasn't sure what he was talking about. I had assumed that the idea of starting up a restaurant together was no longer on the table. Then it suddenly hit me. He had been waiting four whole years! My experiences in Peru and Alaska had made me extremely wary of entering into partnerships with anyone, but his willingness to wait showed me that I could trust him.

In the end, four of us signed a partnership contract: restaurateur Drew Nieporent, investor Meir Teper, De Niro, and myself. Drew Nieporent had not only opened the Tribeca Grill with De Niro but had also founded the highly successful Montrachet, a restaurant considered to be cutting-edge even for New York. His knowledge of the restaurant business and his breadth of experience was amazing, and I recognized in him a true professional even at our first meeting. The chef at his restaurant was selected by *Food & Wine* magazine as one of America's ten best new chefs in 1989, the same year that I was chosen. Later, it occurred to me that Drew must have known about me before we met and might even have encouraged De Niro to convince me to work with them.

Drew and De Niro found a building, and Nobu New York was established in the Tribeca district. Although that area still seemed rather bleak to me, it was just a stone's throw from De Niro's home. I suspect that, in the beginning, De Niro didn't intend to make Nobu this big. Perhaps he just wanted to enjoy the taste of Matsuhisa in his own neighborhood.

WHEN THE TIME IS RIPE, THERE IS NO ANXIETY

People flock to New York from all over the world in pursuit of their goals, and the city is charged with an energy and excitement that is quite a contrast to the more laid-back Los Angeles. I was surprised to see how distinctive the cultures of these two cities were, despite being located in the same country. When I hopped into a taxi at the airport in New York and told the driver where to go, I got no answer. His silence seemed to say, *I know where I'm going. If I didn't I'd ask.* When I dropped in to a Japanese restaurant near where we planned to open ours and introduced myself, the owner said, "See you in six months," which appeared to mean, *New York's no pushover. Let's see if you survive even half a year.*

In the early 1990s, the city was notorious for its cutthroat competition. As the Japanese saying goes, New York businessmen wouldn't think twice about plucking out the eyes of a live horse. Restaurants designed by architect David Rockwell were becoming all the rage, and restaurateurs produced not just the menu but the entire space and dining experience. Those restaurants that survived were best described by the word "professional"— every element from service to the interior decor was faultless. I sensed immediately that New York wouldn't be an easy place in which to succeed. But I also felt that if our restaurant did make it here, it could make it anywhere.

Matsuhisa had only recently expanded from 38 seats to 65, but Nobu New York seated over 150. Although this meant venturing into the unknown, the timing felt right, and I had no qualms about starting something new. The scars from my experiences in Peru, Argentina, and Alaska seemed to have vanished. Working with professionals to create a new restaurant in New York was stimulating and fueled my desire to work harder than ever. A positive tension seemed to course through my veins.

A PRO SYSTEMIZES THE KITCHEN

Drew handled restaurant management. The PR and personnel departments were both part of his company, and as he was top in the field, I could leave all that in his hands and just focus on the sushi bar, the kitchen, and the dining room.

To get ready for the opening, I hired two new sushi chefs and spent six months thoroughly training them at Matsuhisa. Although they were already well versed in the basics of sushi making and Japanese cuisine, my recipes are original, and therefore I taught them by cooking with them. We also advertised for chefs in New York, and many experienced people applied. One of these was Masaharu Morimoto, who went on to star in both the Japanese and American versions of the *Iron Chef* TV series.

When the restaurant first opened, I stayed in New York to train the kitchen and sushi bar chefs. After about three months, things settled down, and, for the next half year, I spent two weeks in Los Angeles and two weeks in New York. In America, people who work on both the East and West Coasts and travel back and forth are called "bicoastal," and it made me happy to realize that I was now bicoastal, too. The best chefs from Matsuhisa also became bicoastal, spending three-month stints in New York training the chefs while working alongside them in the kitchen and sushi bar.

Nobu New York was triple the size of Matsuhisa. This meant changing our approach to every procedure, even from the very first step of prep work. In New York, everything was systematized for maximum efficiency. The kitchen was divided into different areas, such as the salad section, the grill section, and the fry section, and all of the areas worked together to produce a single dish. For example, when making New Style Sashimi, the chefs at the sushi bar would thinly slice the fish. This would then be passed through to the kitchen where the fry section would sprinkle it with yuzu, ginger, chopped scallions, and soy sauce, and then drizzle it with hot olive and sesame oil. In the case of Soft Shell Crab Rolls, the fry section deep-fried the crab first, and then passed it through to the chefs at the sushi bar to make the rolls.

IF YOU STRIVE PASSIONATELY TO COMMUNICATE, BROKEN ENGLISH STILL GETS THROUGH

Matsuhisa's manager also came to help prepare for the restaurant's opening, and together we explained the menu to all the staff. I would begin, describing in my broken English not only how each dish was made, but also how it came into being and the

At Nobu New York with Drew and De Niro.

thought that had gone into it. The manager would then convey the same thing in fluent English.

Notes from these sessions were written up as a collection of stories. The origins of Squid Pasta, for example, became something like this: "One day a boy came to Matsuhisa. He couldn't eat squid. Then Nobu . . ." It would probably have been more efficient for me to speak in Japanese and use an interpreter, but I think that despite my poor English, my passion reached my listeners because I spoke from my heart. This, in turn, laid the foundation for the Nobu Style.

In addition, all the servers sampled the different dishes. Although we had never tried this at Matsuhisa, tasting was done almost daily at Nobu New York. It may seem a waste to prepare dishes especially for the staff, but this step was an important part of the training program developed by Drew's company. Just as seeing is believing, so is tasting. Servers can't explain a dish with confidence if they haven't tried it. This training was applied thoroughly, even to the newest serving staff. Once again, I was impressed by the professionalism of Drew's team.

YOU CAN'T DO YOUR BEST WHEN YOU'RE FEELING STRESSED OUT

In the early days of our partnership, Drew and I once clashed. As an expert in restaurant operations, he is very particular about things like costs and wages. This is an area of weakness for me, so I was extremely grateful that he handled these aspects. At the same time, however, he tended to push things through without considering the feelings of those who worked on the ground.

It was Drew who decided such details as daily sales and turnover targets, but the figures he came up with were quite severe. It's easy to come up with numbers, but it's the chefs and dining room staff who have to meet those goals. When people are constantly stretched to the limit, stress inevitably builds up. I worked side by side with the chefs in the kitchen and even napped with them on the couch during breaks, so I knew instinctively that they were feeling pressured. No one can do their best when they feel stressed out, and guests will pick up on those feelings as well. This approach went against everything I had valued at Matsuhisa. The restaurant in New York bore my name, Nobu. While it was bigger than Matsuhisa, I still wanted to create the same environment, one in which we could enjoy our work and remain intensely focused on the job at hand.

I went to Drew and told him, "People aren't robots!" He gave a snort of laughter, and that made me mad. "Look," I said seriously. "I know this isn't Matsuhisa. I'll try to understand your way of doing things, so please try to understand mine." In the end, he did. Working with Drew was also a great opportunity for me to learn about things like cost, which I had never stopped to consider at Matsuhisa. I'm glad I didn't hold my peace just because Drew happened to be a very successful restaurateur. If I hadn't confronted him at that time and shared what was on my mind, the spirit of Matsuhisa might never have been carried over to Nobu, in which case I believe that Nobu would never have evolved to its present level.

CHANGING THE IMAGE OF JAPANESE RESTAURANTS

Nobu New York opened in August 1994. When summer comes to the city, people often escape to suburban beach resorts or the Hamptons, and the restaurant business slackens off, but not at Nobu. We had a full house from the very first day. Many of Matsuhisa's regulars were bicoastal, flying frequently between New York and Los Angeles, so when Nobu opened, they immediately made reservations. Their presence was a major reason for our success.

I was thrilled to find that the menu concepts I had developed at Matsuhisa still worked, despite the difference in scale and environment. Every time I saw this, I felt like smiling. It was a new and different joy from the thrill I had experienced when Matsuhisa first opened.

Architect David Rockwell's innovative design also contributed to the buzz about Nobu New York. At my request, the interior decor for the dining room featured a cherry blossom motif, ranging from blossoms still in the bud to those in full bloom. The building, which was originally a bank, had a large space that had once been a safe separated by a heavy door, and that's where we decided to put the bar. Almost all the Japanese restaurants in New York were decorated in a style that Westerners considered "traditional Japanese." This included strings of paper lanterns and crimson handrails. Rockwell's Nobu design revolutionized people's image of a Japanese restaurant.

The guests that frequented Nobu New York were even more glamorous than those at Matsuhisa. People often dressed casually when they came to Matsuhisa because West Coast culture is quite easygoing. The space at Nobu New York, however, was very stylish, and guests tended to dress up. Even the presentation of Matsuhisa signature dishes was more refined and evolved. Nobu New York took everything I had done up to that point and raised it to a professional level.

AN EMERGENCY CALL FROM NEW YORK

Hollywood celebrities that were regular guests of Matsuhisa also began frequenting Nobu New York. One funny episode I remember concerns the model Cindy Crawford. Once, when she visited Matsuhisa in Los Angeles, I made her *kakiage-don*, which is mixed tempura on a bowl of rice. She had never tried it before and was thrilled. "What's this?" she asked.

I didn't know how to translate the Japanese word *kakiage-don* into English, so I said, "Let's call it 'Cindy Rice.' " That made her even happier.

The problem was that Cindy happened to visit Nobu New York while I was in Los Angeles. She ordered "Cindy Rice," but, of course, the staff had no clue what she meant. I received a desperate phone call from New York. "What's 'Cindy Rice'?" I was asked. Laughing, I explained that it was mixed tempura on rice, and Cindy went home happy.

Hollywood celebrities are used to being treated like stars. At Matsuhisa, however, we always treated them like any other guest, and those who liked that kept coming back. There is a bond of trust between us, like that between good friends. Having such a strong connection with many of our guests is, I believe, one of Nobu's strengths.

MY GUESTS' SMILES MEAN MORE THAN MICHELIN STARS

Nobu New York's reputation spread as critics came and wrote articles for the *New York Times* and other papers. Drew and his company made good use of these for publicity. Food critics try out our food, form an opinion, and write about it. That's their job. Some are bound to find that my cooking isn't to their taste, but this is no reason for concern as long as the majority of guests who eat my food think it's delicious. Critics are really just the same as any other guest. The only difference is that their opinions might end up in a paper or magazine.

In the same way, I have never been concerned about Michelin or Zagat ratings. Some chefs may aim for Michelin stars, and that's fine. Everyone has their own aspirations and their own approach. But I personally don't seek that kind of recognition for my work. When Nobu New York received a Michelin star, it didn't make me want to strive for more. What brings me joy is seeing my guests smile. What matters most is making my guests happy.

Making my guests happy, however, doesn't mean that I'm aiming to be liked by all of them. Our policy around smoking is a good example. When Matsuhisa opened in 1987, almost every restaurant allowed smoking as a matter of course, and, at first, we did, too. But with only thirty-eight seats, Matsuhisa was tiny. A smoke-filled dining room might be okay for smokers, but I had quit smoking myself and could imagine how unpleasant it might be for nonsmokers. Matsuhisa simply wasn't big enough to make separate smoking and nonsmoking sections, and, about two or three months after we opened, I made up my mind to ban it. When I informed my guests about the new no-smoking policy, a few of them stomped out in disgust and vowed never to return. A few years later, however, the state of California banned smoking in all restaurants. Sales reportedly dropped an average of 35 percent in restaurants within the state, but Matsuhisa was not affected at all. In fact, those guests who had vowed not to come back were now regulars. The no-smoking policy in the dining rooms of Nobu restaurants worldwide dates back to this period.

Some people complain that Nobu is expensive. Perhaps they wouldn't feel this way if they understood that we use no processed foods, select only the choicest ingredients, and don't seek to make an exorbitant profit. Regular guests keep coming back precisely because they do understand.

I NEVER FORGET MY ROOTS—MATSUHISA

Both Nobu New York and Matsuhisa were always full, but the atmosphere of the 150-seat Nobu was completely different from that of Matsuhisa, which originally had only 38 seats. Nobu New York seemed very posh due to the stylish nature of New Yorkers themselves and also to its proximity to De Niro's production office, which resulted in a star-studded clientele. Consequently, Nobu New York was soon the talk of the town.

We had four phone lines for reservations, and they rang constantly from nine in the morning until five in the evening. We only accepted reservations one month in advance, and the restaurant booked up so quickly that we had to apologize to most callers that we were already full. People complained that it took months to get a reservation, and it was a standing joke that when you called Nobu, the response was not "Hello, this is Nobu," but "Hello, this is No."

We served three hundred to four hundred guests a night, and it made me very happy when our system had developed to the point that they all went home satisfied. The professionalism that allowed Drew and his company to manage such a large-scale restaurant so flawlessly was impressive. It could not be run like Matsuhisa. In a restaurant that seated 150 people, for example, it would have been impossible to provide Matsuhisa's ad-lib *omakase* style. We therefore limited this style to the sushi bar and provided a set Omakase Course designed by the chefs for the tables. In addition, whereas dessert at Matsuhisa was limited to fresh fruit, Nobu New York employed a pastry chef who developed such popular dishes as the Bento Box, a chocolate fondant with ice cream served in a lacquer box.

While on the one hand, we needed to evolve in ways that worked best for Nobu New York, we also needed to retain the same friendly, personal, high-caliber service offered at Matsuhisa. For that reason, I was determined that we would never introduce any mechanical, assembly-line approaches. The further Nobu has spread around the globe and the more it has become known and loved, the greater this determination has grown. Thanks to this, Nobu has inherited the Matsuhisa philosophy intact.

For me, Matsuhisa's existence is huge. Whenever I feel uncertain, Matsuhisa is where I return to find my roots. Which is why I have kept that first restaurant in Los Angeles pretty much the way it was in 1987 when it opened. I believe that I did the right thing by taking the time to focus on building Matsuhisa a solid foundation instead of rushing into a new venture with De Niro when he first approached me. If we had opened Nobu New York before I had established the Matsuhisa style, I think that neither would have developed to this extent. The new venture

Matsuhisa in 2013. It still looks the same as when it first opened. The left side became part of Matsuhisa in 1990.

succeeded precisely because the staff at Matsuhisa had been so well trained that I could leave Los Angeles with complete confidence and spend weeks at a time in New York.

VENTURING INTO THE WORLD OF MOVIES

Meeting De Niro literally changed my life, and in more ways than one. Before we met, it never occurred to me that I might one day appear in a Hollywood movie.

The first was *Casino*. This was when De Niro and I were still discussing the idea of opening a restaurant in New York. Apparently, he recommended me to Martin Scorsese, and the casting director called me in for an interview. Being totally ignorant about the movie industry, I told her very frankly that I wouldn't be available to film on certain days because I had to work at the restaurant. She burst out laughing. "Nobu," she said, "this is a major film featuring stars like Sharon Stone and Joe Pesci, you know! We have to arrange our schedule around theirs." That's how clueless I was.

Soon after, I received a call from De Niro's production office congratulating me on getting the part. The film was shot in Las Vegas, and when I reached the site, I found that I had my own trailer in which to relax until I was needed. I could even order in food or anything else I wanted. De Niro, whose trailer was nearby, dropped in with a bottle of champagne and allayed my stage fright by reassuring me that he'd be right there and I had nothing to worry about.

I thought that everyone was treated this way, but in fact, only stars were given their own trailers. When I returned to Matsuhisa and shared my experiences with some of our guests who were involved in the movie industry, they looked puzzled. "A trailer?" they asked, probably wondering why an amateur like me would have one. It wasn't until the next shoot that I discovered my mistake. Bored with waiting in the trailer, I happened to wander around between takes and came across a large tent. It was filled with actors and crew members having lunch. Only then did I realize the special treatment I had received, all thanks to De Niro, of course.

PURSUING A SINGLE JOB CAN BROADEN YOUR HORIZONS

Not long after this experience, Steven Spielberg and Mike Myers visited Matsuhisa with their wives. "If you're doing any movies, give me a call," I joked. Mike Myers, however, actually suggested me to director Jay Roach for a part in the third Austin Powers movie. When they heard about this, the regulars at Matsuhisa insisted that I should do it, so I accepted. I played Mr. Roboto, a character that even had some lines, and I was given an English coach to help me practice. Thanks to that movie, I became pretty famous.

One day, a father brought his young son to Matsuhisa. "Look," he told him. "That's the man who played Mr. Roboto in the Austin Powers movie." Austin Powers was especially popular with kids, and when the boy heard this, he froze and couldn't bring himself to look at me. "Enjoy the food," I said. As I walked away, I could feel his eyes boring into me. I spun around, trying to catch his gaze, but he immediately looked away. I took a few more steps, then turned again. He looked away. His expression was so funny that I couldn't resist doing it again and again. That seemed to help him relax, and he went home looking very happy and content.

Since then, I've had several opportunities to appear in movies and commercials. Experiencing this unknown field was a great education. It was also good publicity for Nobu restaurants. My true vocation is, and always will be, cooking, but by following that calling, I received these offers. I wasn't consciously seeking them, but I think that devoting myself to my profession led to people inviting me to try new things, and that in turn broadened my horizons.

5

Conveying the Taste and Service of Nobu to the World

—

What to keep and what to adapt to the locality

NO NOBU WITHOUT DE NIRO

Nobu restaurants now exist on five continents. Although Nobu Tokyo as well as most Nobu restaurants in the States are under the direct management of our company, the rest are not. This doesn't mean, however, that they are franchises. Our approach is to have the local partner supply the location, staff, and capital wherever the restaurant happens to be situated, be it London, Dubai, or elsewhere, while De Niro, Meir, and I provide the menu and service. We sign a license contract with the owner in each location.

I receive a salary for my work as a chef, royalties for the use of the Nobu trademark, and a certain sum commensurate with the profit made by each restaurant. Seen from our local partners' perspective, the business model means inviting Nobu, a well-known brand, to their area, investing in it, and making income from the profits. Opening a new restaurant involves no financial risk for me or De Niro. The greatest risk we face is the damage a bad partner could inflict on the reputation of the Nobu brand. For this reason, the choice of partners is extremely important. We receive offers from around the world, but negative experiences in the past have made us very careful.

Nobu London, our next venture after Nobu New York, opened in 1997 in the Metropolitan Hotel overlooking Hyde Park. At the time, Nobu New York was still one of a kind, and we had not yet perfected our scheme for global development. Or, to be more accurate, it had not yet even occurred to us to establish Nobu restaurants all over the world. Our London partner, who had been a regular at Matsuhisa for many years, initially wanted to enter into a partnership with just Drew and myself. He did not see the need to include De Niro. While there was nothing to stop me from signing a contract on my own, it was De Niro who had given me the opportunity to open the first Nobu, and I could not imagine entering into a partnership without him. I agreed to the venture only on the condition that the partnership include De

Niro, just as with Nobu New York. Since then, De Niro and I have always been a set whenever we open a new Nobu.

NOBU LONDON STAYS OPEN FOR CHRISTMAS

Once we had decided to open a Nobu in London, I made the rounds of the city's sushi restaurants and found that they had a very limited menu. The only types of sushi offered were salmon, shrimp, squid, and scallop. At first, I thought that these must be the only fish available, but when I visited the fish market, they not only had tuna, but also sardine and mackerel. I realized that the chefs simply couldn't be bothered pickling these kinds of fish in vinegar. This fueled my passion to share the delights of good sushi with people in England.

Just as I had done when we opened Nobu New York, I spent a whole month in London after the opening, making sushi and working in the kitchen as I trained the chefs. Then, when things settled down, I switched to spending two weeks in Los Angeles, a week in New York, and a week in London. Likewise, we began sending, one at a time, the new chefs from Nobu London to train at Matsuhisa and Nobu New York, while the chefs from Nobu New York also took turns working at Nobu London to provide on-site training. In addition, Drew and his team made a handbook that detailed how I had come to open Matsuhisa and how Nobu signature dishes had been born. This was distributed at an all-staff meeting before the opening and used as a textbook on Nobu Style.

When the Christmas season rolled around that year, the manager told me that we would have to close during the holidays because nothing in London stayed open, but I asked him not to. The restaurant, I told him, was in a hotel that would have guests staying through the holidays. If everything else closed down, then there would definitely be people to feed. We stayed open, and, as a result, Nobu was completely full during the holiday season. This experience confirmed my belief that while it's important to adapt to local ways, stepping outside convention is often just as good for business operations as it is for inspiring new recipes.

I remember how thrilled I was to see the dishes that I had invented at Matsuhisa being produced identically in New York, and again in London. I couldn't keep a grin from spreading across my face whenever I ate at either location. I frequently joined my staff after work for drinks and shared with them my dream of introducing the delights of sushi and the wonders of Japanese cuisine to the world.

The next restaurant we opened was in Tokyo. That was in 1998. For me, it represented my triumphant return to Japan, the land where I had been born and raised, and I was deeply moved. Today, Nobu Tokyo is located beside the Hotel Okura in Toranomon, but the original location was in Minami Aoyama. We introduced valet parking, which no other restaurant in Tokyo had adopted. There was also a cigar bar with cigar boxes signed by many celebrities and a garden-style patio lush with flowers and shrubs. Guests who kept up with the latest trends in Tokyo loved these features, and many foreign movie stars dropped by after film premieres.

But even though our restaurant was booming, some of our local partner's other ventures failed, and the company went bankrupt. I couldn't bear the thought of Nobu Tokyo disappearing with it. I consulted Meir, and we decided to open a new Nobu in Toranomon under the direct management of our company and with the New York management team at its core. Like its forerunner in the Minami Aoyama district, Nobu Tokyo is frequented by young entrepreneurs who drive the Japanese economy, as well as by executives from many foreign firms. Nobu Week, when I am there in person, is held once a month and is a very special occasion. Now that I have more time, I like to stop and chat or share a drink with those guests who come specifically to meet me.

GOING STRAIGHT TO MR. ARMANI HIMSELF

The opening of Nobu Milan in 2000 proved to be a challenge for me. Our partner was the internationally renowned fashion designer Giorgio Armani. We were introduced by our London partner, who was in the apparel and accessory business. It took me some time, however, to agree to a partnership, and I ended up keeping Mr. Armani waiting for a whole year.

I think one of the things that held me back was the fact that Italy as a nation treasures its native cuisine. Italians pride themselves on their food being the best in the world. I love Italian cooking myself, but it seemed to me that Italy's food culture could represent a significant hurdle. In addition, Japanese restaurants in Milan only served what Westerners considered classical Japanese food; dishes like tempura, teriyaki, and sukiyaki. I wasn't sure that Nobu Style Japanese cuisine would catch on.

There was another reason for my reluctance. Mr. Armani had once invited me to a fashion show in which he presented designs that combined Japanese and Chinese elements, but his fusion of the two made me wonder whether he really understood Japanese culture. This made me less confident that he would understand my approach.

After a year, however, I decided to give it a try. As I had expected, contract negotiations didn't go as smoothly as they had for New York or London. For instance, one of my conditions was that the restaurant should be nonsmoking, just like other Nobu restaurants. But Milan is a city of tobacco lovers. Armani's negotiators responded that a no-smoking policy was unthinkable. No matter how much we discussed this point, we got nowhere. Finally, I asked them to let me speak to Mr. Armani directly, and I was given a chance to explain in person. As a result, we agreed to allow smoking at the bar in the lounge on the first floor but not in the dining room on the second floor. The world-famous Armani had listened to the philosophy of this simple chef and understood.

The city of Milan enthusiastically embraced Nobu cuisine. A few years ago, I stopped in at a seafood restaurant that had recently opened there. To my surprise, they served a dish very similar to sashimi. When I had first visited Milan, there was no custom whatsoever of eating raw seafood. I asked the chef, "Do people in Milan eat raw fish now?"

"You must be kidding," he responded. "When you opened your restaurant, you changed the food trends in this city, you know."

EXPERIENCED NOBU STAFF TEACH OTHERS

Up until about 2000, I was directly in charge of training the staff for each new Nobu, including those in London, Tokyo, and Milan, as well as for the new Matsuhisa in Aspen, Colorado, which was run under a different type of partnership. After that, our approach changed because by then we had many well-trained chefs and had begun perfecting a scheme for opening new restaurants.

In each restaurant, the Nobu team is organized under the general manager, the sushi chef who runs the sushi counter, the executive chef who oversees the kitchen, the front of house manager who is responsible for the dining room and captains, and the back of house manager who is in charge of inventory. More recently, we have also added the position of corporate chef, a person responsible for the kitchens in all the restaurants within his region.

Work is distributed among these sections, each headed by its own leader. When we open a new restaurant, we bring in experienced staff from other Nobu restaurants to fill the most important posts and to teach the new staff. For the first few months, we also gather a task force of experienced trainers from other Nobu locations to help with staff training. During this process, some of the local employees will demonstrate exceptional ability, and, when thoroughly trained, can take over the key posts so that we can confidently leave the new restaurant in their hands.

I think that it is because I continue to travel to every Nobu restaurant and share my philosophy that Nobu has spread around the world and gained an ever-expanding following of loyal fans; that the food and service at every Nobu is consistently as good as, or better than, Matsuhisa's; and that every member of our staff takes pride in producing Nobu Style food and offering Nobu Style service to our guests. I am always aware that the Nobu brand would be destroyed if I ever took it for granted.

Good food, good service, and teamwork: I am always reminding Nobu staff to focus on these. Good food means putting your heart into your cooking and using carefully selected ingredients. Good service means personal service, practicing the Japanese art of perception to anticipate what each guest wants before they even say it. Teamwork means that everyone, from chefs to general managers, works together as equals.

Although we teach the chefs at every restaurant to faithfully reproduce signature dishes that are served worldwide, such as Black Cod with Miso, we must leave the fine-tuning of the seasonings to the judgment of each chef. After all, each country and culture has its own preferences when it comes to such things as the amount of salt or chili pepper used in a recipe. To ensure that such variations do not stray too far from the original, however, the corporate chefs and I visit every Nobu around the world.

Most large restaurant chains use detailed manuals to ensure uniform flavor, but at Nobu we don't go that far. Perhaps we would need that kind of manual to control quality if our goal were merely to expand the number of Nobu restaurants. But personally, I believe that food should be made by people; it should never feel mechanical. No matter how big Nobu becomes, I want it to keep that quality of being handcrafted, to make sure that it still retains my spirit. In the end, it is not manuals or recipes that determine the flavor, but the chefs, and, while I know that I'm exaggerating, I think that when chefs pour their heart and soul into creating a meal, it will still taste good, even if they mistake sugar for salt.

While the dishes served at Nobu are all part of the style that I created, there is still room for our chefs to express their own creativity. We take pride in offering food with this kind of personal touch. And it can lead to changes that I myself could never have anticipated. That is why Nobu cuisine continues to evolve.

When Nobu chefs come up with new dishes, some of them

inform me conscientiously, while others don't. Nobu sauces and dressings are based on Japanese cuisine, and if a chef uses these when coming up with new recipes, the results will rarely deviate from the Nobu Style. Gregorio Stephenson, a chef at Nobu Malibu, for example, originally trained in Italian cuisine. Utilizing this background, he invented an artichoke salad. While at first glance this might appear to be un-Japanese, the dressing is made with yuzu juice and Nobu brand Dry Miso, which means that any Japanese person would instantly recognize it as having a Japanese flavor.

CREATING NEW TASTES

Cuisine is always evolving. This is not limited to Nobu. Fifty years ago, for example, people used to discard *toro*, the fatty meat from the tuna. No one used sea urchin or salmon roe in sushi, either. The caliber and creativity of a chef is demonstrated by the ability to utilize newly discovered ingredients and techniques.

A case in point is the story behind the invention of Dry Miso, a Nobu signature seasoning made of freeze-dried granulated miso that we sprinkle on things like salads and sashimi. One day, I opened the fridge in my New York apartment and found that the lid had been left off a package of miso. The surface was hard and dry. Most people would have discarded the stale crust, perhaps feeling a little guilty about wasting it, but instead, I took a nibble. It was crisp and quite tasty. When I returned to Matsuhisa in Los Angeles, I began rolling out miso and letting it dry. When I sprinkled a little on sashimi and then drizzled it with olive oil and yuzu juice, the flavor was quite different from that of fish dipped in soy sauce.

But it took time to make this dried miso. Sun-drying took about a week, and even oven-drying took a whole night. I could make enough to use at Matsuhisa with these methods, but not more than that. I was still pondering this problem when I was contacted by Hikari Miso, a manufacturer in Nagano Prefecture that was very eager to sell me their products. Their miso was made with organically grown soybeans and was free of additives or preservatives. At Matsuhisa, however, I had been using one brand of miso in my recipes for a long time. To switch to another brand would impact the flavor of all the dishes that called for miso. I could not possibly change brands. The company, however, was so passionate in their sales pitch that I found myself thinking about what other ways I might be able to use it.

Black Cod with Miso was a signature dish so I could not use a different miso for that, but perhaps miso soup . . . I tried it and discovered that it was delicious. Then, suddenly it hit me—dried miso! I contacted the sales representative and explained that I was currently experimenting with a particular idea and that if they would be willing to dry the miso for me, I would use their product. I am sure they must have been surprised by this suggestion, but they had a freeze-drying component in their factory and, within a few weeks, presented me with dried miso. I love it when people act quickly like this. Hikari Miso has been manufacturing our Dry Miso ever since, and it is used as a seasoning in Nobu restaurants worldwide. Our miso soup is also made with Hikari Miso.

To return to my point, in the past, no one would have thought of using dried miso as a seasoning to sprinkle on salads and sashimi. The more orthodox might protest that sashimi should only be eaten with soy sauce and wasabi, but I believe that there are endless possibilities for evolution in cuisine.

Sashimi Tacos is another example of such evolution. Tortillas and tacos are common in Mexican cuisine, but no one had ever considered using them in Japanese cooking. Curious, I made some mini taco shells and filled them with chopped sashimi, such as tuna or salmon, making sure that the sashimi remained the star. I dubbed them Sashimi Tacos. Tacos are a Mexican soul food, and Los Angeles residents with Mexican roots found them irresistible. Nobu chefs in each area have come up with their own local variations. In Miami, for example, they use wonton shells instead of tacos, while in Malibu they fill the tacos shells with meat cooked in a soy-based sauce.

JAPANESE CUISINE IS THE HEART OF NOBU STYLE

Many people refer to my cooking as "fusion," but personally I don't see it that way. I would rather people called it Nobu Style. Japanese cuisine forms the bedrock of my cooking. I pride myself on having added spices or flavors that aren't part of our traditional cuisine but that allowed Japanese food to win a worldwide following. But what exactly is Japanese cooking? What makes a particular cuisine part of any one nation's culture?

This is a difficult question to answer. Personally, I think that a cuisine unique to a certain country or culture is one that utilizes the umami distinctive to that region. Umami is an internationally recognized term for a savory taste discovered by a Japanese scientist. Parmesan cheese, for example, would be the umami of Italy. I often tell Nobu chefs to study umami carefully.

In Japan, we make *dashi*, a soup stock extracted from such ingredients as kelp and bonito flakes. It forms the basis of all flavors used in Japanese cooking. To this are added basic seasonings, such as salt and sugar, and sometimes a few spices. Together, these provide the basic framework for Japanese cuisine. Nobu Style is based on Japanese *dashi*, but with restaurants on five continents, I enjoy discovering ingredients that represent the umami native to other regions, using them to develop new recipes, and incorporating these into our menu. It is my firm grounding in Japanese cuisine that allows me to do this. In my opinion, cooking that lacks a clear foundation is confusion, not fusion. I call my approach to cooking Nobu Style because it is Japanese cuisine that belongs anywhere in the world.

WHY I SPEND TEN MONTHS A YEAR TRAVELING AROUND THE WORLD

Some people might be puzzled by the fact that I spend so much time and effort traveling to every Nobu restaurant. It would seem more efficient to make a complete Nobu Style manual that explained my approach. But that wouldn't work. Many aspects can't be expressed in words alone. If I tried to force them onto paper, those words would take on a life of their own, and before I knew it, Nobu would no longer be Nobu.

That is why I take great care to communicate my ideas directly to our staff, and not just in words. I demonstrate with passion and then let them try it. I want them to pick up the things I teach by feeling them rather than by thinking about them. This is why I spend ten months a year like a traveling missionary, going from one restaurant to another to communicate the Nobu philosophy.

At every restaurant, I start off by sitting down at the sushi counter and asking the chef to make me two or three pieces of sushi. As soon as I taste it, I can tell immediately if the rice is too tight or too loose, can detect how the chef's hand has shaped it, and can determine whether or not the toppings have been pre-pared correctly. The ingredients, such as the type of rice and vin-egar, and the recipe, including how to prepare the seasoned vin-egar, are standardized, but the taste and texture of the sushi will change with the weather conditions and any slight alterations in the chef's handling of the ingredients.

Once, I noticed that a chef had applied a little too much pressure to the rice. There was no air between the grains, and this made it dense and chewy. The man had had almost twenty years' experience as a sushi chef and had joined Nobu eight years earlier. "The rice is too dense," I said. He looked startled. I later learned that the restaurant had been so busy, he had started pushing himself to work faster. My comment had made him aware that rushing was causing him to squeeze the rice. Sushi rice should be gently molded in the hand to keep air between the grains. This is the most basic rule of sushi making. He was shocked to realize he had forgotten to keep this in mind, but I later heard that he was very happy I had told him, which, of course, made me happy, too.

Japanese cuisine, on which Nobu Style is based, makes the most of Japan's four distinct seasons, featuring ingredients and flavors specific to each. I encourage Nobu chefs to learn about these and then to explore and develop their own variations. Another distinguishing feature of Japanese cuisine is that the dishes on which it is served often have one side that is considered the *shomen* or "front." I don't think this concept exists in the West, or at least, I have never noticed it with plates used for such Western dishes as pasta or pizza. In Japanese tea ceremony, for example, the teacup is always presented with the front side facing the guest. To show humility, the guest then turns the cup slightly to avoid drinking from the front. Again, in the West I haven't seen this kind of sensitivity and attention to detail so typical of Japanese hospitality etiquette. I ask Nobu chefs to keep these concepts in mind when they are preparing food for our guests.

For example, sashimi should be arranged quite differently on a plate for only one or two people sitting at the counter than on a plate intended for a table of four or five guests, in which case it will be viewed from all sides.

Many people will never notice such things, and there is no need to explain. But when we take care of such details as a matter of course and someone who does understand notices, then this effort becomes a thing of great value.

WHY I PAIR LOCAL CHEFS WITH NATIVE JAPANESE CHEFS

Food is fleeting. It's gone within seconds. First, it delights the eye, and then, the palate. The chopsticks move busily, until all that is left is an empty plate. This is a chef's greatest joy. We use our creativity to invent dishes that our guests will consume with pleasure. That is how Nobu signature dishes such as New Style Sashimi and Black Cod with Miso were born. While some criticized these as not being pure Japanese cuisine, my guests embraced them as Nobu Style. My stance is to stay firmly rooted in Japanese cuisine while adding innovative touches so that people in a particular location can enjoy my food.

Still, there are certain dishes that will never be included in the Nobu lineup. There is a line that cannot be crossed. This standard, however, is hard to explain.

When Nobu opened in Hawaii, the local chefs decided to

come up with original dishes as ideas for our menu. One of them used sausages in his recipe, but from my perspective, sausages and Nobu Style are completely incompatible. Not only are sausages un-Japanese, but they are a processed food, and that is not the Nobu taste. Therefore, regardless of the kind of sausage used or how it's presented, it can never become a Nobu dish. We do have seafood dumplings in Japanese cuisine, so fish sausages handmade by the chef in the restaurant might be considered Nobu Style, but I would never think of using store-bought sausages. Serving anything processed or store-bought is simply not Nobu Style. This is why cheese is only used as a seasoning at Nobu restaurants.

The chef who came up with the idea, however, saw nothing wrong, probably because sausage is such a common ingredient in Hawaii. I told him point-blank that that was not Nobu Style. "Never put fish with sausage," I told him. "You can't taste the fish." He understood what I meant and continued to develop. A year later, he came to Nobu Los Angeles as a junior sous chef. I was surprised and delighted to see him, but I didn't know his name yet. "Sausage Boy," I said, "what are you doing here? No sausage on my fish, right?" His name is Jason Benavente, and he went on to become the executive chef of Nobu Los Angeles.

This is one of the reasons I always have a local chef and a Japanese chef manage the kitchen of every Nobu. There are some things about the spirit of Japanese cuisine that it takes a Japanese mind to understand. Likewise, it takes a local chef to understand the preferences of the people who live in that region. Having two main chefs who can complement and support each other in this way means that Nobu restaurants can adapt to any location.

My philosophy cannot be passed on as "know-how." But people can grow and change if they are given the opportunity. Lessons gained through a flash of insight become firmly rooted. The only way I can help all of our staff to understand the Nobu philosophy is to continue sharing it until it clicks.

I ASK MY STAFF TO AIM FOR *MY* BEST

In this way, with the occasional mistake, the Nobu menu is continually being renewed. I think this is one of the reasons our regulars love Nobu. They know that anytime they come, they can count on enjoying their favorite dishes and on discovering something new.

New dishes are not created in one go. When a chef comes up with an idea, the first thing I do is taste it. Although my personal preferences will influence me a little, I can still tell immediately if it is delicious or not. Cooking is very truthful. A dish made by a chef who longs with heart and soul to explore new things tastes very different from a dish made by a chef who feels obligated to come up with something new for Nobu to try.

After I have tasted it, I will share my ideas about what I might have done or how it can be improved. Based on this advice, the chef uses his or her ingenuity to refine the recipe and then lets me taste it again. We then repeat this over and over again. For example, Sobagaki, a dish developed at Nobu Tokyo, took over a year to perfect through this process. Sobagaki is really just buckwheat flour kneaded with hot water, but it is very difficult to get the right consistency. Every time I went to Nobu Tokyo, I would taste it and suggest that perhaps it needed to be a little firmer, and the chefs would rewrite the recipe. In the end, the product that gained my seal of approval was really delicious. The perfect firmness will differ from one person to the next. What I consider to be just right is really just my own preference; it's not absolute. But I still ask my staff to aim for what I consider the best. That becomes Nobu Style and spreads worldwide.

I love people who respond immediately to my advice. This makes it easier for me to share my ideas and results in their rapid development. On the other hand, people who respond cheerfully enough, but don't put my advice into action, progress much more slowly, which is a waste. Then, there are some chefs who, even when I give them advice, still insist that their recipe is superior. In such cases, I take more time to explain what I would do and why. Every person has their good points. It's my job to draw those out. I don't believe in making people do things my way. Instead, I try to see things from their perspective and find the most effective approach for each individual. The new dishes that other chefs propose are often a source of inspiration for me, too.

Nobu and Matsuhisa restaurants bear my name. They are

like a part of me. But I have no desire to force them to be the way I want. My approach is to let my staff try out things that feel right to them and then bring that together into a unified whole. It's a bit like being the conductor of an orchestra. The musicians are each responsible for their own part, and the conductor, while appreciating their individuality, brings them together as a whole.

According to what I have heard, our staff all love Nobu and take great pride in working there. Nobu as a business has fostered a culture that celebrates diversity, and I think that makes it a more enjoyable and less stressful work environment. Because we give our chefs the freedom to use their own discretion, they enjoy what they do. Chefs who have trained at other restaurants before coming to Nobu have told me, "The work here is never repetitive or boring because we're always thinking together about new menu ideas."

IT'S SELLING, SO WHY WORRY? THIS ATTITUDE CAN LEAD TO MAJOR LOSS

Leaving things up to the discretion of the chefs does have its drawbacks. Nobu Style cooking is based on Japanese cuisine. Although Nobu Style embraces elements that are not found in traditional Japanese cooking, I still want the result to feel rooted in *wa*, meaning the essence of all things Japanese. For non-Japanese chefs, it is particularly hard to judge that fine balance.

That is why I constantly travel around the world to explain Nobu Style. Even so, items that deviate from this style occasionally end up on the menu.

The Nobu in Malibu, California, for example, created the Slider, a small wagyu beef hamburger. It was an instant success, probably because it was so different from the burgers served at fast-food joints in America, the land of bread, meat, and ketchup. But it couldn't be called Nobu Style. While the recipe for the beef patty was good, bread simply doesn't exist in Japanese cuisine. I explained this point passionately to the local chefs and asked them to take it off the menu, but it's very hard to stop something when it becomes so popular. Even if the guests love a dish, if it isn't Nobu Style, the restaurant serving it will no longer be Nobu.

My business partner Meir lives in Malibu. "It's selling, so why worry?" he said. But I felt strongly that this way of thinking could cause major damage when looking at Nobu as a whole.

"If a dish is based on something that isn't Japanese," I insisted, "it's no longer Nobu. No bread!" In the end, he agreed.

That is my role at Nobu now—making sure all our restaurants stay true to the basic tenets of Japanese cuisine.

DON'T BAN NEW DISHES, MAKE THEM BETTER

Gregorio, the chef at Malibu, is an excellent chef and really understands Nobu Style. He was very sorry to have put the Slider on the menu before checking with me and, ever since, has always contacted me whenever he has an idea for something new.

Although I had banned the Slider, I also knew that guests might complain when they saw that it was no longer on the menu. I had to do something. Matsuhisa is my point of origin, and as soon as I returned there, I told the chefs that I wanted to make a Nobu Style slider that was even better than the one in Malibu. Together, we brainstormed about how to make a bun without using bread. We tried replacing it with rice patties, like a rice burger, as well as with a kind of fluffy fish paste called *hanpen*. Our final solution was to combine crushed, well-drained tofu, *yamaimo* (Japanese mountain yam), and some seasonings, shape this mixture into buns, and bake them for twenty to thirty minutes. When filled with a wagyu beef patty and sautéed shiitake, these made an even better burger than the one in Malibu. That was the birth of the Matsuhisa Slider.

NEVER FORGET THE ESSENCE—IN COOKING, SIMPLE IS BEST

Young chefs occasionally surprise me by coming up with difficult and complex dishes that leave even me trying to guess how they made them. When that happens, I ask, "How long do you think it'll take you to make an order of fifteen at a time?" The response is usually a groan.

I know they want to impress me with an artistic masterpiece that showcases all their skills as a chef. But that isn't enough to make a dish professional. It's disappointing when something you've worked really hard on fails to make it onto the menu. At the same time, however, this is how chefs learn that, unlike music or painting, cooking doesn't culminate in the creation of a single dish. You have to make that dish into a recipe that any chef can follow to reproduce the same thing, repeatedly and exactly, even if they get ten or twenty orders at once.

I don't reject the elaborate efforts of any chef outright. After all, I used to do the same thing myself. Instead, I simply share what I would do. I know how it feels to be itching to try new things, and I want them to feel free to experiment. I hope they will discover for themselves through trial and error that the best way is to serve food that is simple with minimal embellishment.

There are countless ways to make food look pretty. When I was young, I garnished dishes with seasonal flowers, displayed food on large, ornately decorated plates, and came up with flashy presentations. There was also a period in my career when I liked to show off my culinary skills. Now, however, my cooking leans increasingly toward simplicity. When I slice two or three pieces of sashimi, arrange them on a plain white plate, and place them in front of my guest, I put all my heart into determining the volume, the timing, and the way I place the dish. It is a personal and impassioned performance for my guests at the counter. I feel as if I have come full circle, returning to the style of a traditional Japanese sushi bar.

I have worked for over fifty years in the world of sushi, and I love it from the bottom of my heart. I see sushi as the height of simplicity, the most profound food in the world. Driven by this love, I have constantly pursued what it means to be a sushi chef. In all these years, this feeling has never changed.

What does it mean to be a sushi chef? It's hard to put into words, but at the very least, I know that it doesn't mean showing off your skills to your guests. Only when you have stripped things down to the bare essentials and eliminated every extraneous detail can you discover the essence of making sushi. Although prep work takes a long time, the actual process of making each piece is very simple: you just gently shape it in your hand and serve it. For that very reason, I want to create the perfect balance of topping, sushi rice, and hand movement, remove any distractions in size, color, or presentation, and bring out the very best in the ingredients.

In any profession, it's only when we have fully grasped its true essence that we can break from tradition. Conversely, if we forget that essence, all our efforts will come to nothing. As long as we assume that success means receiving recognition and praise, as long as our focus remains fixed on the superficial, we will get no closer to the true nature of our work. If we haven't grasped its essence and don't love it from the bottom of our heart, our work will never bear fruit, no matter how hard we try. But once we've found the essence of our profession and start doing it purely for the love of it, our hard work will always open the path before us. That's why I keep traveling the world to encourage our staff to try new things and to remind them never to lose sight of the essence.

6

Transcending a Crisis in Our Partnership

—

Constantly perfecting quality

PULLING OUT OF PARIS

Nobu Paris opened in 2001 and closed in 2003. This was the only Nobu that ever closed due to a breakdown in communication with my business partners. The restaurant itself was great and had a high reputation with our guests, but the approach of the local partner was not compatible with my philosophy.

This strained my relationship with De Niro and Meir as well, and for a while, we became a bit distant. It would be another two years or so before we opened any new Nobu restaurants. It was not that I disliked the restaurant in Paris. It was just that I and the local partner were not on the same wavelength. Nobu is the embodiment of my passion for cooking. If my partner doesn't understand this, then it's impossible to create a Nobu together. This was the lesson our management team learned through this painful experience.

Even though we had to close the restaurant, we still gained something. It was here that we first met Hervé Courtot, who was hired as a kitchen chef when Nobu Paris opened. Hervé had previously worked making French cuisine at a luxury hotel, but he had a strong interest in and a deep respect for Japanese food. He absorbed the Nobu Style willingly and faithfully. When I taught him how to make Japanese soup stock, for example, he weighed each ingredient I used to the last milligram in his quest to replicate the flavor. After the Paris restaurant closed, I stayed in touch with him, promising him that one day we would work together again. In 2008, he joined us in the kitchen of the newly opened Nobu in Dubai.

Dubai is located in the Islamic world, and there are many restrictions on foods, including seasonings. The use of alcohol is also strictly prohibited. Hervé was the perfect man for this job as he had once worked as a chef in a hotel in Dubai. He now oversees the Nobu restaurants in the entire Middle East region, including Riyadh in Saudi Arabia and Doha in Qatar, as well as Nobu Moscow in Russia.

STARTING OVER IN PARIS

My partner for the Matsuhisa restaurants in Greece ran a pop-up in a hotel in Paris. Pop-ups are temporary restaurants that operate for a limited time in one place. The Paris pop-up was manned by chefs from Matsuhisa Mykonos, which is only open from June to September. This team also operated a pop-up in Switzerland during winter from December to March, so the Paris pop-up ran during the spring and fall. It was so popular that we were asked to start a permanent restaurant.

Having failed in Paris once, I was confident that this time around we could succeed. In fact, I had been waiting until the time felt right rather than pushing things. When it comes to ingredients, you can get just about anything in Paris, and the labor market is also very good. In addition, many Parisians like Japan and respect Japanese cuisine. When Nobu Paris opened, the concept of Nobu Style drew much attention. This time, however, I wanted to try something smaller. It seemed to me that the Matsuhisa brand would suit Paris best. Arrangements were made with the Nobu management partners, and Matsuhisa Paris opened in April 2016.

NOBU DOESN'T BARGAIN

America is a contract society. This means that negotiating the details in a business contract is really important. Lawyers include clauses covering everything conceivable, even the fact that you might die. The ambiguity so typical of Japanese culture is taboo. In societies like America's, everything down to the smallest item must be negotiated and incorporated into a contract. To protect Nobu's brand image, for example, we even specify that we will use original Nobu dishware.

I have learned a lot about this process from conducting business in many parts of the world. Just because we've put things in a contract, however, doesn't mean that all we have to do is follow every clause to the letter. Rather, I see the contract as an outline of the bare minimum required. When my partners and I share ideas and collaborate to make Nobu even better, we build bonds of mutual trust that transcend the realm of sticking to, or deviating from, legal agreements. It's almost as if there is no contract. This is why it is so important that my partners understand my philosophy regarding food and service, and that I can accept their way of thinking. This is also why, even when I receive offers from big names in the business world, I will turn them down flat if we can't reach complete agreement. I am quite comfortable doing this because I don't feel any pressure to accept. I have no desire to push forward with a project about which I have any doubts.

Once, during a meeting, a business partner spent so much time talking about financial details that I became a bit impatient.

"I'm not cheap, you know," I told him. This was my way of saying that we should be talking about how to make our guests happy. When we spend all our time worrying about money, we lose sight of the smiles on our guests' faces. He grasped my meaning immediately. "Okay. I get it," he said with a laugh.

I don't like people who take unfair advantage of others, either. The only time I think about money is when considering how much it will cost to do something. I don't want to waste my energy haggling for better conditions. If I had extra energy for that, I would rather spend it on my guests, which is why I also turn down offers from people who try to bargain.

Working with people from many countries and types of organizations, I have come to realize that they each have their own way of doing things. No matter how big the project, the best approach is for the people at the top to talk together. They should share their thoughts and ideas with each other frankly, even if it results in a clash of opinions. There is no point in doing business unless it is to succeed. The same is true for a business in which multiple organizations are collaborating: the main goal should be to ensure that the project succeeds. If a business fails because those involved wasted their time and energy asserting their own share or their own rights, it's because they got their priorities wrong. I have no desire to waste my time guessing my partner's true intentions or having them probe mine.

According to the rules of American society, you have to foresee and include within a contract even the minutest details. It is not only a way to protect yourself, it's a declaration that tells others you're no pushover and that you won't let them get away with unreasonable demands. What I want, however, is different. Instead of using a contract as a shield to defend ourselves from each other's selfishness, instead of insisting on "me, me, me," I want to invite the other person to work together as "we." Negotiations should be about understanding the other party's position while bringing them closer to your own. If we insist only on our own point of view, we will never get anywhere. Even in negotiations, it's important to ask, "What if I were the other person?"

Because I have stuck with this approach, people now know that "Nobu doesn't bargain." And that makes decision making quick and easy.

RELATIONSHIPS WHERE 1 + 1 = 100

In a good partnership, one plus one adds up to a hundred, while a poor partnership can actually result in a minus value. If one or both parties have a bad experience that kills their motivation, one plus one makes even less than two, and it would have been better to have had no partnership at all.

Sometimes I think I have a sixth sense for spotting people who are fixated on money or are trying to take advantage of me. This keen nose for trouble probably developed during my many years overseas. Communicating with my guests or negotiating was a struggle because I didn't know the language. Through this process, however, I instinctively developed ways of communicating that didn't rely on speech alone. Perhaps my internal radar is more sensitive to the meaning that lies behind the words, picking up cues from such things as gestures and facial expressions. If so, it's a very precious tool.

When I am planning to open a new restaurant, I always go to the site to check out such things as the availability of ingredients and the location, but a relationship of mutual trust with my partner is far more important than either of these. Take, for example, Nobu Cape Town in South Africa, which is located inside One&Only hotel and has a terrific view of Table Mountain. I first worked with the owner to open Nobu Atlantis, Paradise Island in the Bahamas and Nobu Atlantis in the Palm Jumeirah hotel in Dubai. As both of these were overwhelmingly successful, he then proposed that we open a restaurant in Cape Town, where he was born. The owner of Nobu Budapest, who happens to be the producer of such movies as *Rambo* and *Die Hard with a Vengeance*, was originally a regular at Matsuhisa in Los Angeles. For years, he kept telling me that he wanted to open a Nobu in Budapest, Hungary, his hometown. In the end, we did. Many Nobu restaurants around the world were established through such personal connections, a fact that demonstrates how important trust is for me in a business relationship.

THE GROWTH OF THE NOBU MANAGEMENT TEAM

The painful experience of having to close Nobu Paris actually strengthened the foundation of our management team, which consists of De Niro, Meir, and me. We have gotten very good at carrying out our individual roles while respecting what the others do. Drew became less involved in management after Nobu London, while Meir, who had only been a silent investment partner when we were developing Nobu New York, gradually took on a central role in negotiating with local partners. His experience as a movie producer makes him a highly skilled negotiator, which requires the ability to juggle many interrelated elements.

When we get an offer to open a new restaurant, Meir starts off by consulting with the prospective local partner. If he thinks there is a possibility of doing business together, he contacts me, and I meet with the candidate. If I feel that we can understand each other and work together, Meir leads the way in negotiating the license contract. Once the contract has been concluded, I consult with the chief operating officer and corporate chef about personnel and concrete operational details, including which chefs we can send in and who should be promoted to the position of manager. When it comes time to open the new restaurant, De Niro, who is known worldwide, handles the publicity, appearing on television and being interviewed with me.

IT'S FUN TO WORK WITH PARTNERS WHO HAVE HIGH IDEALS

Larry Ellison, the cofounder of Oracle Corporation, has been a regular since the early days of Matsuhisa in Los Angeles. He also owns the Nobu Malibu building. Originally, Nobu Malibu was located in a mall, but when Larry bought land along the beach, he suggested that we relocate, and we did.

Later, I learned that Larry had bought the island of Lanai in Hawaii. He is, after all, one of the wealthiest people in the world. In the fall of 2012, he contacted me to tell me that he wanted to open a Nobu on the island and asked me to come and see him. He sent his private jet to pick up Meir, our chief operating officer, our corporate chef, and me.

Lanai, which was once a Dole pineapple plantation, currently has a population of around three thousand. It can be reached in just thirty minutes by plane from Oahu and in about forty-five minutes by boat from Maui. Despite its accessibility, however, it retains its natural beauty, and much of the landscape is untouched by development. Four Seasons runs two hotels there: The Lodge at Koele, which is on top of a hill, and The Four Seasons Resort Lanai at Manele Bay, which is located on the coast. We went to see the one on Manele Bay. At that first meeting, we decided the design we wanted, and just six weeks later, in December 2012, the restaurant opened. Sometimes it's possible to open a restaurant that fast, although I have to admit that this case was exceptional. The timing just happened to be

In De Niro's office with Meir.

perfect. The opening of Nobu Hotel had been slightly delayed, which meant that we could send dishes and other things intended for that project to Lanai.

Establishing a Nobu on Lanai was only one part of Larry's plan. His aim, he explained, was to develop an environmentally friendly and sustainable economic model for the world. He even bought an airline, which he intended to use to increase the number of flights to the island and encourage more visitors to come. Other plans included developing local renewable energy sources and the infrastructure for electric cars. Larry also described his dream of protecting the island's ecosystem by making shelters for its teeming population of stray cats, and encouraging ecotourism to provide local jobs.

It was very clear to me that Larry wasn't interested in development for the sake of short-term profits. Instead, his passion was directed toward high ideals. This made me want to contribute in whatever way I could. I proposed setting up a vegetable garden to grow produce and fish farming facilities to raise fish for the Nobu restaurant. If we produced a surplus, we could start a weekend farmers' market. It might even be fun to include food stalls.

Less than half a year after the restaurant opened, we launched Nobu Garden at Bennie's Farm under the capable leadership of Nobu Lanai's executive chef at the time, Oyvind Naesheim.

WHEN A NOBU OPENS, THE TOWN CHANGES

After choosing a good partner, the next most important thing is choosing the building. I always go to the site myself and look it over very carefully. While I'm there, I imagine what kind of Nobu the place would become. If the image that comes up is a good one, then I'll take it. I have only my intuition to rely on. I either get a feeling that it will work—or that it won't. I know it will be a sure success when I can visualize which chefs would do a good job in that particular location and can see the smiling faces of the guests seated inside.

People often say that when a Nobu opens, the whole town changes. This idea arose from a comment that Madonna made, but I think it's true. With the establishment of Nobu New York, for example, the run-down warehouse district of Tribeca livened up. When Nobu London opened on Old Park Lane, a street lined with luxury hotels, it raised the level of other Japanese restaurants in the area. Similarly, I have heard that the service in restaurants in the Bahamas improved after we opened a Nobu there. The Bahamas is quite laid-back, and servers usually think nothing of making their customers wait. Nobu's spirit of thorough service, however, changed what people in the local service industry had once accepted as common practice. One of our London regulars who happened to visit Nobu Atlantis in the Bahamas praised it lavishly the next time he saw me and declared that the service was even better than Nobu London's. Little did he know that the London manager happened to be right beside me. "You've got to be kidding," the manager muttered, and then lapsed into a stunned silence.

TRUE COMPETITION LETS RIVALS COEXIST AND PROSPER

When I open a restaurant in a new location, my goal isn't to become the sole winner. Imagine if a new Japanese restaurant were to open down the street from Nobu. Most people would see this as the start of a fierce competition for clientele. But I don't. I see it as a favorable development that will raise the prestige of Japanese cuisine in the whole area by generating a competition to produce the best quality. Instead of trying to beat or make more profit than someone else, the real contest is to do our best for the sake of our guests. True competition increases the quality of both parties. With this kind of competition, rivals can coexist and prosper together.

I don't remember feeling this way in Los Angeles, which is a sprawling city with lots of room between the buildings. I think I first became aware of it when we opened Nobu New York, where the crowded quarters generate a high level of competition among restaurants. If we don't consciously seek true competition, which develops the level of all involved, it's impossible for a restaurant to grow.

WAITING UNTIL THE THREE KEY PLAYERS ARE READY

The three key players in the management of a Nobu restaurant are the manager, the chef, and the sushi chef. I cannot open a new Nobu until we have developed these core members. People can start up as many restaurants as they like as long as they have a place, but no one can start up a Nobu without personnel who understand the Nobu philosophy. This is not something that can be learned simply by reading a manual. I can only entrust a new Nobu to people who have worked at one and have experienced my philosophy firsthand.

From 2005 to 2009, the number of Nobu restaurants increased at a rapid pace. We opened new restaurants in Dallas, on Fifty-Seventh Street in New York, on Berkeley Street in London, in Hong Kong, Waikiki, Melbourne, San Diego, Los Angeles, Dubai, Cape Town, Moscow, and Mexico City. People were impressed, but personally, I was uneasy. It felt too fast. No matter how well things seemed to be going, I knew we couldn't do everything at once. Team building is particularly important. Even though business was going well, I felt that we would risk compromising quality if we kept expanding the number of restaurants before building up a solid team. We would run out of people qualified to serve as core members and would be unable to train new ones. As a result, the quality of our food and service would inevitably decline.

I bear almost no financial risk when we open a new restaurant because the Nobu business model is a license model. If I had wanted to get rich, I could have just accepted every offer I

At the opening party for Nobu Dallas.
(Photo by Steven Freeman)

received and continued expanding the number of Nobu restaurants indefinitely. But in doing so, I felt that I would lose something very important—the trust of my guests that I had nurtured since the first Matsuhisa. Without that, Nobu would quickly disintegrate. Nobu is my name. I was very conscious of what that meant. If I became cocky and pushed ahead carelessly with a new restaurant before I was ready, my name would be tarnished. That would be like cutting my own throat. At a meeting in New York, I told my business partners that it was time to pause and focus on raising the quality of our existing restaurants.

I frequently receive multiple offers to start up new restaurants, and if I only cared about making restaurants in form alone, I could make as many as I wanted, as long as I had the money and a location. But I don't see any point in making a new restaurant if I can't put my heart and soul into it. I decided not to give the go sign for any more restaurants until I felt we were ready. By that, I meant having enough time to be properly involved on-site and being able to train the staff, particularly the key players.

THE IMPORTANCE OF REPETITION

As of November 2017, a total of forty-seven Nobu and Matsuhisa restaurants have been established worldwide. My job now is to further enhance their quality. Interviewers often ask me what my favorite restaurant is, but wherever I go, I almost always eat at a

Nobu. If I notice something that needs attention, I'll immediately pop into the kitchen to offer advice. If the presentation isn't quite right, I'll call the chef over and suggest how it could be done better before I even pick up my chopsticks.

I can't check the quality of every Nobu restaurant all the time, but I can generate a constructive tension among the staff by eating at each Nobu whenever I can and repeatedly giving feedback. Through this process, the chefs begin to notice things for themselves as they work. This is how I raise up chefs with a good understanding of my cooking.

At every Nobu restaurant, I always repeat the same things: *Good food, good service, teamwork. Put your heart into your work and cook with passion. Do whatever your guests want as much as possible and make them happy. Your guests don't come just to eat. Put your heart into giving your guests the best experience from the moment they walk through the door until the moment they leave.* I repeat myself constantly, so that very soon the chefs and the manager are saying the same things to the rest of the staff and this way of thinking permeates the whole restaurant.

WHY I'M ALWAYS WILLING TO TAKE PHOTOS WITH MY GUESTS

Wherever I go, Nobu staff will almost always use my visit as an opportunity for promotion. They'll come up with a theme, such as "Sake Dinner." Many people will specifically make a reservation for that day because they want to see me. As much as possible, I visit each table to greet every guest. Often servers will come to me and say, "Nobu, would you stop at that table next, please?"

Smartphones have made taking photos easy. When I visit a table, the guests are likely to ask, "Can we take a photo?" Of course, I say yes. They'll take one, and then say, "Oh, I forgot the flash." They'll take another, then decide to try a different angle. Quite often, I end up posing for three or four photos just at one table. Although, to be honest, it can be quite tiring, I still do it with a smile because it makes our guests happy. And not just our guests. It makes the servers even happier, because they want to see their guests go home smiling. I think my willingness to respond with a smile to the wishes of my guests inspires the same attitude in my staff.

WE DON'T NEED A MANUAL FOR HOSPITALITY

The word *omotenashi* refers to the Japanese spirit of hospitality or service. This is the consideration that everyone working at the restaurant shows the guests and each other. If the servers merely perform each task mechanically—welcoming the guests, guiding them to a table, giving them a menu, taking their order, serving the food, and bringing them the bill—it's not a real restaurant. We should tailor our interactions to each individual guest at that particular time on that particular day, including what we say when we greet them and take their order, the timing and delivery of the food to their table, and the type of conversation we have with them. Rather than just doing these things as a routine, we should constantly be attuned to their needs and provide the very best hospitality at each particular moment. Manuals can't make a restaurant. Rather than relying on a manual, we should constantly be asking ourselves, "What if I were the customer?"

Excessive service is not good hospitality, either. The idea that you can have too much of a good thing applies to serving, too. For example, if a guest has only taken a single sip from their glass of water, it's not good service to immediately fill it up again. Although some restaurants might say in their manuals that servers should fill a glass before the customer has finished their water, the best timing is to wait and fill the glass the moment it's empty. Or actually, to wait until the glass is empty and then to sense whether or not the person wants more, and decide what to do on that basis. Just the simple act of filling someone's glass as soon as they want more can make our guests feel comfortable.

The same applies to pouring tea. In Japan, it is proper etiquette to fill the *yunomi*, or teacup, about 80 percent full. As Japanese teacups don't have handles, this makes it easier to pick it up without spilling the tea and also keeps the brim from getting too hot. Because many Nobu employees are not Japanese, it's only natural that they wouldn't know the right amount of tea to pour for their guests. I teach them by example, pouring them some tea and letting them drink it. This way they can learn through experience.

I can't possibly give all my guests this much attention on my own. But many people work at Nobu restaurants, and if they all approach their work with this attitude, everyone will be taking care of the guests, and the guests will love being there. Sometimes, after careful thought, we may decide to do things differently from what our customers want. But as long as we do so with complete sincerity, they will understand. No matter how many times we say "I love you" those words will mean nothing if we are insincere; when said with feeling, they will always reach the other's heart. With this kind of service, our guests will go home happy, word will soon spread, and more people will come.

Restaurant turnover and profits are important in business. But for me, it is of even greater value to bring smiles to our guests' faces through consistently offering good food and service and a space to enjoy a pleasant conversation over their meal so that they always leave satisfied. Like the wheels on either side of a car, good food and good service are inseparable. Even if the food is superb, no one will want to come back if the service is lousy. That's how important service is, even though it has nothing to do with cooking. Instead of making a manual or developing a training program to spread my philosophy, I explain these points carefully to our staff at every opportunity. This may seem like a lot of work, but in the end, it's actually the easiest way.

WHEN YOU HAVE TO REPRIMAND STAFF, PUT YOURSELF IN THEIR SHOES AND CHOOSE YOUR WORDS CAREFULLY

Visiting Nobu restaurants all around the world is a lot of fun, but it can also be frustrating. Sometimes I see ways of cooking that go against my philosophy or service that is lacking in consideration. Even at Matsuhisa, my starting point, I occasionally find that something important has changed when I return from an extended absence. When that happens, I begin by asking why they changed it. If they can give me a good explanation, they might convince me that the change is for the better. But if they can't, then it's a problem. In that case, I will tell them very sternly that it doesn't make sense to change the way we have always done something if they can't explain why. Matsuhisa is the origin of every Nobu restaurant. We need to have a very good reason if we're going to change the approach we've followed so carefully all these years. There is nothing wrong with change. But when we make a change, it must be for the better.

At the same time, there's no point in getting so angry with staff that they feel terrible. If they seem slow to respond to my questions, it often means that they're reluctant to point out someone else's mistake. That's why I never single out one individual. Instead, my approach is to improve overall teamwork. I address everyone, speaking from my heart so that they can feel how serious I am. This prevents anyone from feeling hurt or ashamed. Besides, if I tell five people and even one of them takes my words to heart, he or she may then encourage everyone else to try what I have suggested. When a problem occurs, it's important to address it openly and discuss it together. Then no one feels personally attacked or criticized, and the team can share their opinions constructively instead of searching for where to lay the blame.

BEING AN EXAMPLE IS MORE EFFECTIVE THAN REPRIMANDING

There are some people who continue to speak harshly to others even after working with us for some time. In such cases, I give them this advice: "When you say it like that, you could hurt the other person's feelings. Instead of telling them in words, think about how you can be a good leader and show them what they should be doing by your own example." Again, it all depends on how I say this. Telling someone off without giving them a chance to explain won't make the problem go away. I need to put myself in their shoes and think about what I can say or do to make them want to change. If, as a result, they actually do change, then that makes both of us happy.

Telling someone what to do very rarely results in the other person being able to do it right away. It's fine to make mistakes. We can learn from them, and that will help us to advance, step by step. Fortunately, at Nobu, there are now many people who can provide support if anyone slips up. Of course, carelessness is not acceptable, but if someone makes a mistake while trying to do their best or because they took on a new challenge, others will always help them out. At Nobu, I believe we've managed to establish a culture where anyone who tries their best and isn't afraid to make mistakes can win distinction.

As long as we learn from them, mistakes are never a waste. Sometimes, however, people will repeat the same error over and over again. I might want to say, "Give me a break!" but I rarely need to. The fact that our staff all have the Nobu spirit and work together as a team has a sort of self-cleansing effect. When someone makes an error, he or she will pick up on the vibes and notice quite quickly without having to be told. People who repeat mistakes because they simply aren't trying hard enough usually leave the team of their own accord.

YOU CAN'T TEACH SOMEONE TO HAVE A "HUNGRY SPIRIT"

Guests from all over the world send me comments about up-and-coming Nobu staff. A regular at Nobu Malibu, for example, might write to praise one of the younger chefs. I make sure to pass this kind of comment along because I know it will make that chef happy and inspire him or her to try even harder.

Not so long ago, a chef with quite a bit of experience joined Nobu. I knew that for this very reason it might be challenging for him to get used to working with us. The menu is extensive, there are many Nobu Style ways of doing things, and the level expected is very high. But I received messages, one right after the other, from guests who had sat at his counter on different days. Both of them commended him very highly. I told him immediately. "Always remember how you feel right now," I said, "and keep doing your best. If you do, your efforts are bound to lead to success." It makes me very happy, too, when guests compliment my staff. Just like kids, we all need praise to grow and develop.

At the same time, if we are to grow of our own volition, we must experience that frustration which makes us determined to master something no matter what. This feeling, however, has to come from within. Otherwise, it's meaningless. A hungry spirit is the one thing that no one can teach us. And it only dwells within those who are determined to succeed no matter what. I am what I am today because I was determined to grasp every opportunity that came my way, no matter how small.

ALWAYS THANK THE DISHWASHERS

In my case, everyone knows that I can cook, so they will listen to my advice. Leadership is easy when the leader has the knowledge required. But when a business expands, it becomes impossible for that person to stay on top of everything. Managers with no cooking experience may have to give instructions about the food. If they aren't careful, they could end up offending the chefs. This is why people who become leaders must study. They don't have to learn how to cook, but they must make the effort to understand how those who are cooking feel. If they do, everyone will follow them. On the other hand, if they boss people around just because they're the leader, no one will. That's why I always tell people in the position of leader to work twice or even three times as hard as those who work under them.

Gratitude is also important. If the plates are dirty, chefs can't present the food. Dishwashing is a very hard job. The people who do it risk cutting their hands, and the soapy water can chap their skin. When I travel to different Nobu locations around the world, I make a point of thanking the dishwashers. People at the top of any business should spend time with their staff in the workplace, working alongside them so that they can understand how they feel. If they do, the people who work for them will be more likely to understand their feelings and be willing to try even harder.

Don't waste time thinking about whether you know or don't know, about whether you can or can't do, something. Start by doing, by putting thought into action. It is this attitude that gives an organization energy. The most important role of a leader within any organization is to create this kind of business culture and raise up the next generation of leaders.

7

Heading into a New Stage
—
Launching Nobu Hotel

FROM RESTAURANTS TO HOTELS

Las Vegas, Miami, Dallas, Hawaii, Melbourne, Cape Town, Hong Kong, Beijing—all the Nobu restaurants in these cities are located inside luxury hotels. In addition, De Niro, who owns the Greenwich Hotel in New York, has close connections with the hotel business. According to him, when a Nobu restaurant opens in a hotel, the hotel's reputation rises. As a result, Nobu also becomes more popular. Nobu restaurants and luxury hotels seem to be very compatible. Based on that,

De Niro proposed the Nobu Hotel project. Instead of opening a restaurant in someone else's hotel, he suggested that we make our own.

I am the type of person who always works directly in the field. From this perspective, even opening a single restaurant seems like a huge job. Although the project team would include experts in hotel management, I would be lying if I said that I had no qualms at all. At the same time, however, I was deeply moved to think that, in just fifteen years, Nobu had developed the capacity to realize such a project. For this reason, I decided that it was worth the challenge.

The project team traveled all over the world, researching and negotiating, until we finally came up with a plan to renovate one of the towers of Caesars Palace in Las Vegas. It had taken us about five years from the time the project team formed to reach this point. This first venture was not a stand-alone hotel. Instead, we transformed 181 of the 2,000 rooms in the Caesars Palace tower into the Nobu Hotel. Of course, it housed a Nobu restaurant, too, the concept for which was created by a team led by corporate chef Thomas Buckley and myself. Hotel management was handled by Caesars Palace, which kept our risk in that area relatively small. Still, the scale of a hotel is different from that of a restaurant. I felt energized and excited, just like when we were launching the first Nobu while I was still running Matsuhisa in Los Angeles.

REFLECTING NOBU CONCEPTS IN HOTEL SERVICE

Although we used the staff and know-how of Caesars Palace for hotel management, the service concept for Nobu Hotel was designed by Nobu Hospitality, a company we established to direct our expansion into the hotel business. Meir, De Niro, and I each played a key role in the company's management, and Meir, in particular, was very involved in negotiating a broad range of issues with Caesars Palace.

The structure was similar to our approach with Nobu restaurants, in which we provided the concept and the expertise while the local owner actually ran the business. The interior design was entrusted to the Rockwell Group, which had already designed many Nobu restaurants, including Nobu New York.

We began by taking particular care in choosing the bedding because most people spend the majority of their time at a hotel sleeping. Based on our experiences traveling around the world, Meir and I advised on what kind of beds, pillows, and sheets provide the best night's sleep. The comfort of the bed and bedding was not our only focus of concern. Meir and I had both experienced the inconvenience of needing an extension cord in order to plug in our smartphones and laptops by the bedside. The layout of electrical outlets was thus another important consideration.

The design concept was Japanese-style, and we therefore replaced slippers with *zori* sandals woven from toweling, and bathrobes with light, cotton kimonos known as *yukata*. I wanted to put a Japanese Washlet, the most advanced toilet in the world, in every room, but in the end, due to budget considerations, we limited these to the suites only.

Speaking of Washlets, a TOTO sales rep came and installed one in Matsuhisa Los Angeles just when we were first becoming popular. I'm sure he thought it would be great publicity because many of our regulars were celebrities. People who used the toilet would come back to their seats and say, "Nobu, great!" We were always running out of the TOTO business cards we left in the washroom, which shows how much our guests loved that toilet. Like Japanese cuisine, the Washlet is a fine example of Japanese artisanship and attention to detail.

We made the sinks at the hotel quite deep. Sometimes I like to wash a few things by hand when traveling, and it's much easier to do that in a deeper sink. I wanted to install a Japanese bath in every room, too. The Japanese bath is a deep soaking tub that overflows when you settle into it. The floor of the bathroom has a drain, and you wash yourself outside the bath before getting in. Once again, however, the budget wouldn't allow it. Instead, I settled for placing a wooden stool in each shower room. In the West, people stand up to take a shower, but Japanese are used to sitting down to wash, so we decided to introduce that approach. Although we had to give up on installing Japanese baths in Las Vegas, this is a dream I hope to realize in the future as we continue to create more hotels.

WELCOMING OUR GUESTS WITH JAPANESE TEA AND *SEMBEI* CRACKERS

The person mainly responsible for deciding hotel operations and detailed furnishings was Gigi Vega, vice president of Caesars Palace and general manager of Nobu Hotel. With twenty-four years of hotel management experience, she is an expert in service. She listened intently to what I had to say and worked extremely hard to make sure that the Nobu Style permeated the hotel. Even when choosing such little details as the soap and shampoo, for example, she asked me what kind of scent I liked. "I really only care about how food smells," I said, "although I prefer everything to be simple." She then had soap and shampoo samples made with different blends of ingredients that fit her image of "simple" and personally tried them out, finally choosing a delicate scent called "rosemary and white tea."

In each room, guests arrive to find Japanese tea and a Nobu original teapot to welcome them. This is a custom I picked up from Japanese inns, which always provide tea and sweets in the room. At Nobu Hotel, instead of sweets, we offer Japanese rice crackers called *sembei*. I happen to love *sembei*, perhaps because Sugito, the town where I was born and raised, is famous for its *Soka sembei*. I decided to serve these packaged in an original Nobu wrapper. Made from rice and basted with soy sauce, they are very crunchy and flavorful.

To serve these *Soka sembei* at the hotel, however, I needed to import them. I contacted several *sembei* manufacturers in Sugito, but none of them believed me when I said I wanted them for a hotel in Las Vegas. When I asked them to send a sample, they refused, thinking it was some kind of scam. I didn't know what to do. A junior high school classmate, however, happened to know the third-generation owner of a *sembei* shop called Hayashiya. It makes me quite happy to think that by creating Nobu Hotel, I can now give something back to my hometown.

For many Japanese, I think that *sembei* is the taste of home. Yet even though it is so representative of Japan, this snack is not well known elsewhere. That is another reason I chose it as a way to welcome our guests: I wanted to introduce it to the world. It would be fun if *sembei* became so popular that it inspired someone in America to try making something similar.

The minibar in each room contains Hokusetsu sake and Matsuhisa's original wine. When staff usher guests into their room, they explain that these are Chef Nobu's choice.

TWENTY-FOUR-HOUR NOBU ROOM SERVICE

Breakfast, as a rule, is served in the room. The guest orders from a room service menu that includes such traditional Japanese fare as *yudofu* (lightly boiled tofu) and grilled fish. But limiting the menu to conventional Japanese dishes would be boring, so I decided to come up with something that anyone anywhere can eat yet is

Welcome tea service with Japanese tea and sembei crackers.

Shower room.

Deep sink in the washroom.

still very Japanese. The result was the Scrambled Egg Donburi. No matter where you go in the world, hotels always serve eggs for breakfast. In Japan, they also always serve grilled fish and nori seaweed. My breakfast bowl combines all of these ingredients in one dish. I lay toasted nori on rice and then add a layer of flaked grilled salmon. I top all of this with scrambled eggs and a sprinkling of *ikura* (salmon roe). Because this is a hotel, we also offer Western-style dishes, but we add a Japanese touch even to these. Our green tea waffles, for example, are extremely popular.

Room service is offered twenty-four hours a day. The chefs work in three shifts of eight hours each in the kitchen. None of us at Nobu had experienced this shift pattern before. But I saw it as an opportunity for our chefs to expand their potential. At first, our corporate chef, Thomas Buckley, and our executive sushi chef, Takahiro Otomo, faced many challenges, such as coordinating operations with the executive chef responsible for overseeing all of the many restaurants within Caesars Palace. But I kept encouraging them. It's up to each individual to grab the opportunity, I told them. Great achievers are people who can learn from any situation and make that knowledge their own. That's what it means to have a "hungry spirit."

ONE MANAGER'S COURAGEOUS DECISION

We reassigned many of those employed at Nobu Las Vegas in the

Hard Rock Hotel & Casino to the restaurant in Nobu Hotel. Chef Otomo was promoted from second sushi chef at Nobu Las Vegas to Nobu Hotel's executive sushi chef, while Annie Kim, who had worked for many years as the Nobu Las Vegas general manager, became general manager of the new restaurant. The Nobu at Nobu Hotel, however, was very different from any other Nobu restaurant. Not only did it seat 374 guests, but it also offered breakfast and room service. Coordinating service to the hotel rooms added on a large-scale operation that we had never had to deal with before. When it first opened, the restaurant was booked so full that some of the guests staying at the hotel were unable to eat there. Realizing that the scale of this new stage was a little too large for her to handle, Annie asked the chief operating officer, Fumihiro Tahara, better known as Hiro, to demote her. When Hiro consulted me about her request, I recognized this as a courageous decision on her part and, wanting to support that, agreed to accept it. Her decision wasn't made from a concern for appearances or for what others would think, but rather from an understanding of what was best for the restaurant and also for herself.

I promoted Bryan Shinohara, who had been working under her, to the position of general manager, and moved Annie to second-in-command. For Bryan, the promotion was a priceless opportunity, and he worked to take full advantage of it. Annie, who had asked to be demoted, took charge of operations within the restaurant, and has been doing a great job. I think that this incident further broadened her perspective. Now, it is as if we have two very capable managers. An organization in which everyone does their best makes it possible to assign staff flexibly like this so that everyone can grow.

If we try something new but find that the challenge is beyond our ability, it's okay to take time out to build up our skills and then try again. If we keep on trying, we will definitely learn to do it. People like Annie, who recognize their lack of ability and take the time to develop it, who strive to make the impossible possible, will always grow and develop. On the other hand, people who throw in the towel as soon as something doesn't work out can never accomplish anything. Life won't always be smooth sailing, so when adversity strikes, just tell yourself that you've returned to your starting point.

I entered the world of cooking at the age of seventeen. I spent the first three years at the bottom of the heap, washing dishes, making deliveries, cleaning tables, and pouring tea. I believe that I have become what I am today because of this experience. If I had skipped that stage, I might have become one of those owners who doesn't understand the feelings of their staff. Nor would I have developed the ability to supervise every part of the operation.

Often, we only become aware of the value of such experiences much later. There are countless examples of people for whom an experience at the time was nothing but agony, yet who now look back on it with gratitude. No experience is ever wasted.

When climbing from one level to the next, we might, in our haste, be tempted to skip a step instead of taking them one at a time. But if we miss that step, we may never have another opportunity to gain that experience. Even if it slows us down, taking each step one at a time helps us to truly grasp the value of everything we need to reach where we are going. Personally, I don't think racing up the stairs is always the best way to get somewhere.

No matter how big the organization, people who are chosen as leaders share certain qualities in common. I am not talking about ability or achievements. Rather, it is a bit like choosing who will be the class rep in elementary school. What counts is whether or not that person is someone others want to follow. It is when timing, character, and passion coincide that a person emerges as a leader. When someone is not chosen, this doesn't mean that his or her capacity isn't recognized. It just means that at that particular time, there is something else that person should be doing.

A RESTAURANT WHERE YOUNG EMPLOYEES THRIVE FEELS GREAT

In Nobu restaurants today, there are many stages at which our employees can shine. I personally think we've built a great system that allows people to step up their careers by identifying their next goal and working toward it. And I think this is the result of carefully fostering the development of each individual restaurant.

For me, the ideal restaurant is one where junior employees are eagerly learning and progressing, not one where I can boss people around. Young people who are working hard and developing quickly will listen intently to every little piece of advice. This makes me want to teach them more, and they, in turn, develop even further. If there is even one employee like this in a restaurant, all the rest will be swept along, until everyone is advancing their skills and feeling great about it.

If you want happy staff, the key is good communication, not money. When someone listens empathetically, it makes us feel good. Such a relationship of trust inspires us to strive even harder. It's impossible to build a true organization with a management approach that relies on money as the sole incentive for staff improvement. Although money helps us to make a living, it can never make us happy.

PIONEERING NEW THINGS IS ALWAYS MET WITH CRITICISM

Our first hotel opened in Las Vegas. But it did not have to be there. We might have been just as successful if we had opened one in New York. It is not the location that matters, but how hard we strive to make sure that later we are glad that we started it where we did.

Many people have criticized me for venturing into the hotel business. Some have warned me not to assume that my success with restaurants will translate over. I see this as a kind of baptism, one that can't be avoided when attempting something new.

I guess that no chef before me has tried their hand at the hotel business. But I have been through this process many times before.

The Japanese sake, Hokusetsu, which is loved by Nobu guests the world over, is a good example. When I started serving it, no one believed that this sake, which was little known in Japan, would one day be enjoyed worldwide. Recently, we have begun serving it in wineglasses. This actually started in 2008 at the Matsuhisa restaurant in Greece when we were doing a Sake Dinner promotion. Traditionally, sake is served in a ceramic flask called a *tokkuri*. People tip the sake into little cups, or *ochoko*, usually pouring for each other. I felt, however, that if we wanted to make sake better known to the rest of the world, we needed to upgrade its image. Pouring chilled sake into a wineglass not only makes it classier, but it also allows our guests to enjoy the bouquet, just as they would for wine. In addition, it makes it more accessible to women, allowing them to drink it with elegance and to experience its flavor. If this style spreads internationally, we will have contributed to the dissemination of Japanese sake. I see no reason not to try something a little different when it has such great potential.

Our custom-made *chirori* is another example. In Japan, these small metal kettles were traditionally used to heat sake at the hearth. Again, in the beginning, no one believed that these would be used by Nobu restaurants throughout the world. Originally, we used bamboo vessels to serve sake. These were imported from northeastern Japan, but due to the impact of the earthquake

With De Niro at the opening of Nobu Hotel in Las Vegas.
(Photo by Erik Kabik)

and tsunami in 2011, we could no longer obtain them. Although that was very sad, I was determined to turn misfortune into opportunity. I therefore arranged for artisans in the Tsubamesanjo region, which is famous for its metalworking technology, to make an original *chirori* for use at Nobu restaurants.

We are very fortunate to have many discerning guests who understand the difference in the quality of what we offer. Nobu can now serve as a vehicle to naturally introduce superior products to the world without the need for advertising. We simply incorporate these things as part of Nobu service. I think that this is one of the great attractions of the Nobu brand.

DEVELOPING ORIGINAL TABLEWARE TO CONVEY JAPANESE CONCEPTS

At Nobu, we have been making our own original tableware since 2003. Before that, we ordered all our dishes from a commercial provider. A manufacturer, however, proposed that I develop my own brand. This idea caught my interest. When Matsuhisa was still the only restaurant I ran, I once designed dishes with a morning glory motif. It was a set of five plates, beginning with a morning glory in the bud. As the meal progressed, the morning glory gradually unfurled until by the fifth and last plate, it was in full bloom.

My first design for Nobu was a plate that would not be marred by fingerprints. No matter how clean a plate is, it is bound to acquire a fingerprint or two along the way when we place food on it and carry it to the table. I had always hated the thought of that fingerprint marring the plate while our guests tried to enjoy their meal. I therefore hit upon the idea of giving the edge of the plate a matte finish so that it would not show any fingerprints. I also came up with designs for a series of dishes with pine, bamboo, and plum motifs, as well as a clock plate design and a simple oval-shaped plate.

Unlike conventional Western-style plates, these designs all incorporated the concept of *shomen*, the Japanese word for "front." The fact that there is meaning even in the direction in which a dish is placed is the quintessence of Japanese cuisine, and I wanted to express this in the design. The clock motif was a convenient way of demonstrating the concept of a "front" to people who don't know Japanese culture. Just saying "six o'clock" helps them to understand.

I came up with many more designs after that, including a plate just for Black Cod with Miso and an extremely simple yet functional sushi plate with an indentation for soy sauce. Almost all Nobu tableware is white. I think of plates as a canvas to which the chef can freely add color. Plates with gorgeous designs may overpower the food, and that would be a waste.

All the Nobu restaurants use the tableware I designed, which means that you can eat the same cuisine from the same plates anywhere in the world. This makes it easier to maintain the consistency of the Nobu brand.

A THANK-YOU LETTER FROM A CRUISE PASSENGER

The partnership with Crystal Cruises, a project launched in 2003, presented us with a series of challenges. We put a Nobu Style sushi bar aboard a luxury cruise ship that traveled the world. Crystal Cruises proposed the collaboration and installed a sushi bar inside Silk Road, one of the ship's restaurants. Hiroshi Nakaguchi, a sushi chef who had worked with me for many years since the time of Nobu New York, was put in charge. I told him that if guests asked for things that weren't on the menu, I would like him to respond as best he could instead of refusing outright. The operation staff, however, protested that this would create mayhem, because at that time, guests on board could only choose from a fixed menu. I explained that as they had gone to all the trouble of asking me to participate, then it made sense to incorporate the spirit of hospitality with which I serve my guests rather than sticking to a fixed repertoire of my recipes.

One day, I received the following letter.

My mother and I took this cruise together. She loves cruises and is quite used to traveling by ship, but this time, she began feeling a little under the weather. When I told

Mr. Nakaguchi, he brought a bowl of udon noodles to our room. He had made the broth from scratch. Thanks to that, my mother recovered quickly, and we were able to enjoy the rest of the trip. We've decided that next time we travel by boat, we'll take the Crystal Cruise again.

Just a simple bowl of noodles can move a person's heart. As a result of such incidents, criticism of our approach gradually lessened. Instead of changing things just for the sake of change, if you think about what you would want if you were the guest and do your best to meet the needs of each situation, things will naturally change for the better without even needing to worry about it.

In 2013, I offered cooking demonstrations aboard a cruise. Unfortunately, I fell ill and had to get a shot to keep myself going. I asked Nakaguchi to make me a bowl of noodles and a few pieces of sushi. After eating this, I slept for over ten hours and, when I woke up, I was fine. Although we can't fulfill everyone's wishes, I think that we should always want to do whatever we can in response to each situation.

The sushi bar was a success, and guests can now eat Nobu Style sushi on two Crystal Cruises ships: the *Serenity* and the *Symphony*. The sushi bars don't take reservations, which means there is a line every day before opening, and the seats fill up as soon as the doors open. Recently, I have noticed quite a few children of various nationalities at the sushi bar. They seat themselves at the counter and order Soft Shell Crab Rolls or *kappa maki* (cucumber rolls). This shows how well known sushi has become, and that makes me very happy.

A SPIRIT OF MUTUAL LEARNING, NOT RIVALRY, MAKES ORGANIZATIONS STRONGER

Nobu restaurants are always trying new things, and employees make full use of mailing lists, Skype, and other means to share their successes with staff at other Nobu locations. It's Nobu culture for everyone to work together when implementing a new idea. I'm very proud that we work as a team, rather than trying to sabotage each other's efforts.

In the food industry, chefs are normally very protective of their kitchens and most would never send their staff to work at branches elsewhere. At Nobu and Matsuhisa, however, sushi chefs, kitchen chefs, and managers go overseas on business trips and may even be posted to jobs in other countries.

In the summer of 2013, for example, we did a Nobu promotion in Monte Carlo. The Cannes Film Festival and the F1 Grand Prix were being held at the same time, so we did a pop-up, bringing in staff from Dubai, Miami, New York, Dallas, and Aspen. This generated an exciting chemical reaction. Sushi chefs, kitchen chefs, and managers from different restaurants matched skills, exchanged information, and inspired and stimulated each other. I know that the experience will help them to grow. Although it was only for one month, they also formed strong bonds and have stayed in close contact ever since. This network represents one of Nobu's invisible assets. The promotion was so well received that negotiations to open a Nobu in Monte Carlo went very smoothly, and we opened in December of the same year.

The Nobu restaurant aboard the Crystal Cruise ships could be called a "Nobu-in-motion," and that results in some interesting developments. The chef on board might contact me, for example, and say, "We'll be docking at Cape Town soon. Can you ask the chef at Nobu Cape Town to prepare some ingredients for me?"

I then put the two chefs in touch with each other. The chef on land will procure local foods and deliver them to the chef on board, most likely along with some tips on how to cook them. It's a source of great joy for me to see chefs who work in very different environments collaborating in this way and holding each other in mutual respect. These moments show me that not only has our business grown, but the Nobu spirit has also developed right along with it.

In general, when a business expands, it becomes that much harder to coordinate and unify. But with Nobu, the spontaneous spread of our staff network, which links every restaurant, has created synergy. The desire to learn from one another is far stronger among our restaurants and staff than rivalry. I think this is the result of creating a business culture that readily welcomes and incorporates new ideas and approaches. For example, if a regular guest of Nobu Atlantis in the Bahamas should request Miso Cappuccino for dessert at Nobu New York, the New York staff will immediately email the Bahamas staff for a recipe and receive it along with a photo. This kind of thing happens daily.

MY STAFF'S SUCCESS IS MY SUCCESS; I WANT THEM TO GRASP OPPORTUNITIES

No matter how large a business grows, its employees are people, not robots. If all we do is make them work, they cannot develop. By focusing instead on how to motivate each individual to strive and grow, we end up generating growth in our business as a whole.

In June 2013, Nobu New York held a Sake Dinner promotion featuring *namazake* (unpasteurized sake) and *yuba* (bean curd sheet). Chefs from many other Nobu restaurants gathered in New York to create new recipes using *yuba* and serve them to our guests. The month before, Nobu Tokyo had also used *yuba* in a promotion, and therefore I asked one of the chefs from Tokyo to come. He shared what had gone well, and what had not, with the chefs gathered in New York. This was a priceless opportunity for them to learn about *yuba*, a Japanese ingredient that American chefs get few chances to experience. At the same time, the Tokyo chef was able to see how our guests in New York responded to the food, and on that basis, to develop the *yuba* recipes even further and reintroduce them to Japan. Being able to offer this type of dynamic learning space is another strength of our current organization.

When chefs are given the opportunity to go on a business trip overseas, there is no point in treating it merely as a chance to sightsee. It's not enough just to come and participate in the promotion, see the Empire State Building, and make friends with the New York staff. What I demand is one or two steps beyond that. I want them to be greedy to learn, to bring back new ideas and knowledge and teach them to the staff back home. By raising the level of their restaurant in this way, they will, in turn, raise the level of their own work. Whatever effort they make will come back to them. Not everyone gets such a precious opportunity, and I always urge those chosen to take full advantage of it.

HAVING CHEFS WHO ARE TEAM PLAYERS IS YET ANOTHER NOBU STRENGTH

I often send young chefs undergoing a spurt in development to promotions and other events. Mixing with top chefs motivates and inspires them. It's a chance to learn directly from the masters and to find role models. This fulfills an important function within the Nobu system for training the next generation.

While it's a great honor to be invited to a gathering of international chefs who are stimulating and challenging each other, it is not enough just to participate. I want these young chefs to be hungry for knowledge, to be determined to take home something new. People who are eager to learn from others pick up far more than those who push others aside in their desire to be number one. And they will continue to advance steadily, because with each step forward, they will see the next step they need to take.

When young chefs come together and share their knowledge, they always come up with creative solutions, even if the challenge they are given is one rank above their current capacity. They become capable of things that they could not have done on their own. That, I believe, is the power of a team. Our ability to raise up chefs who are team players, rather than mavericks, continues to drive Nobu forward. In that sense, Nobu Hotel is the epitome of Nobu Group teamwork, a thought that makes me even happier.

MAYBE I DID IT

At the opening of Nobu Hotel in Las Vegas in April 2013, I had had a little too much to drink and had been showered with congratulations and praise. I got up on stage feeling very good. The crowd greeted me with cheers and applause. I could see the faces of guests from the early days of Matsuhisa and Hollywood celebrities who had come especially for this event. And, of course, our exceptional staff and my family, who have supported me through everything, were there, too. I was filled with emotion. I had been debating what to say in my mind, but braced by the sake, I blurted out, "Maybe I did it."

8

Work Hard with Passion.
The Rest Will Come.

TOWARD OUR NEXT DREAM

We succeeded in going beyond the framework of Nobu the restaurant to create Nobu Hotel. In 2015, we opened another one in Manila in the Philippines, and plans for others are in the works in such places as Chicago and Miami. We have also opened new restaurants in Malaysia and Mexico.

Of course, my goal for all of them is to make our guests smile, but for Nobu Hotel, I also have another dream. I want to use it as a venue for a convention or promotional event bigger than anything we've done before and invite chefs from Nobu and Matsuhisa restaurants around the world, and maybe other chefs with whom I'm good friends. I see it as a grander version of Nobu United, an event we currently hold regionally to bring chefs together from different places within the same area, such as the United States, and have them collaborate on the creation of a full-course meal. If we hold such an event on a global scale, I am sure it will generate something new. I get excited just thinking about it.

In my life, I have tended to just go ahead and try things instead of planning them through carefully in advance, and for the most part, the results have been good. More important than calculated plans, I think we need to have the courage to try something that catches our interest and the determination to do it right once we get started. We don't always need to have a specific reason for doing something. If we just get started, the value of what we're doing will become clear to us later on.

COMMUNICATION IS MORE IMPORTANT THAN A MANUAL

More than twenty-three years have passed since Nobu New York opened. We have thirty-eight restaurants throughout the world. The scale of our business is now so large that I could not possibly oversee the management of all the restaurants on my own. For this reason, in 2012, I appointed Hiro (Fumihiro Tahara) as chief

Nobu United held in Las Vegas. A total of twenty-seven chefs gathered from all over America.
(Photo by Erik Kabik)

operating officer to handle all those aspects that I can't see to properly. Hiro started off as a server at Nobu New York where he demonstrated a capacity for leadership. Although he has no experience with cooking, he has a thorough understanding of my approach and of how I feel, as well as an outstanding ability to put plans into action. He's also quick to respond. Reaction time is very important because, in business, it's crucial to "strike while the iron is hot." In addition, he listens to the staff. Like me, he can put himself in the other person's shoes and act from that perspective.

Efficiency has improved in many areas since Hiro began overseeing all our restaurants. When I come up with a new dish, he immediately spreads it to Nobu restaurants worldwide and adds it to the menu. As soon as a decision is made, he conveys it to all our managers and chefs. Thanks to him, we have significantly improved management efficiency without any reduction in the quality of our food or service. Nor does he force things through. Instead, he improves performance through good communication. He is always on Skype or email, communicating with chefs and managers in various parts of the world, so that sometimes I wonder if he ever sleeps.

This connection to the world means the bigger the business, the more interesting the work. With just a small amount of effort, a huge sum of money moves, and that makes working for a large corporation exciting. At the same time, however, we must never lose sight of the company's roots or the philosophy of its founder. If we condense that into a manual and assume that just by reading it the staff will understand, the future of our business will be limited. No matter how big a company grows, it is important for those at the top to continue sharing their message directly with their employees. I believe that efforts to build any organization, including a company, must be based on person-to-person communication, and not dependent upon manuals or systems.

Manuals and systems never change once they have been made, unless someone deliberately revises them. Communication, on the other hand, is constantly evolving in response to circumstances. The best mode of change for any company is for its leaders to guard their philosophy while at the same time adapting it to meet the needs of new situations and to keep communicating this evolving vision directly to the people who work for them.

I often take Hiro with me when I travel because the best communication is face-to-face. During these trips, I tell him that raising the quality of our existing restaurants is just as important as increasing their number. Without that vision, we will inevitably get off track. We need to keep returning to our founding philosophy. If we don't, at some point we will deeply regret it.

I feel extremely blessed to be working closely with so many young people who understand my thinking 100 percent.

YOU'VE MASTERED YOUR TRADE WHEN YOU CAN RAISE AN APPRENTICE TO YOUR LEVEL

At Nobu, we also have a system for thoroughly training newer chefs and service staff. People currently working as Nobu chefs and managers who have a gift for teaching are sent as trainers wherever needed to thoroughly develop our employees' skills. If we are opening a new Nobu somewhere in Europe, for example, we'll send trainers from London; if we're opening somewhere in Asia, we'll send trainers from Australia. In this way, Nobu staff are often on the move, and Hiro is the main person responsible for coordinating their movement.

Being motivated to learn and paying attention are the most essential keys for personal growth and skill development, but I have come to feel quite strongly that we also need to teach our staff properly rather than just telling them "Watch me and do as I do." Not long ago, for example, we held a sushi making class at Nobu Dubai. More than ten guests applied, which was too many for me to handle on my own. Before the event, I showed the Nobu Dubai chefs how to teach others to shape the sushi rice. Of course, they all knew how to do it, but they each had their own personal style. To make sure we could teach in a uniform manner, I advised them to break it down into six steps. This advice must have clicked, because the way they manipulated the sushi rice improved immediately, and I realized that things I had been doing as a matter of course for years could provide valuable hints to others. I could also see how much a few words of advice helped the chefs relax and gave them confidence. In Japan, apprentices in most trades were given very little verbal instruction. Instead, they were expected to use their brains and "steal" skills from their master and older coworkers through observation. While this is one approach to training, experiences like the one in Dubai have taught me that appropriate advice given at the right moment can trigger dramatic development.

Teaching people requires patience. For a chef who works alone, this is not an issue, but if you want to convey a skill to others, you have to keep at it until they have fully grasped what they couldn't understand before. As long as you are still working from a sense of what feels right, rather than from conscious understanding, you can't explain a skill to anyone else, because you haven't truly mastered it. That's why I think chefs or any other artisans can only be considered full-fledged when they are capable of teaching others. I'm sure that this applies to every profession. And when skills and know-how are shared within the unit of a team, it becomes possible to do things that you could never have done on your own.

YOU CAN COPY MY RECIPES, BUT NOT MY *KOKORO* (HEART)

When Nobu began to spread around the world, I was thrilled to see that the dishes I had created at Matsuhisa were identical wherever I went. Not only that, but restaurants that had no connection with

Nobu began copying my style and serving similar dishes. I have to admit that, as a chef, I felt pretty pleased with myself. When Black Cod with Miso became a hit in London, a local newspaper headline punned, "De Niro is the Godfather, but Nobu is the Cod Father." I also came across a London restaurant that boldly proclaimed on its menu "Salad with Matsuhisa Dressing." They probably got the recipe from my cookbook and included the word Matsuhisa without realizing that it was my name.

There is a restaurant that is actually called Nobu in Kiev, Ukraine. It's a small place with a sushi bar and, of course, has no relation to the real Nobu. It made me laugh when I saw that the menu was exactly the same as ours. People often ask me, "Don't you mind?" but frankly, it makes me happy. Mind you, from a business perspective, it won't do to have people use the Nobu name without permission.

In Moscow, there is a sushi restaurant called Osumosan. When I dropped in, I found that one page of the menu was identical to ours. There is a reason for this. When the first chef we hired at Nobu London left, he was in high demand precisely because he had worked at Nobu. He passed on what he had learned at every restaurant he worked in after that.

At a sushi restaurant in Cape Town, South Africa, I came across soft shell crab rolls. I was very moved to think that this dish, which I had invented at the suggestion of a guest at Osho in Los Angeles, had crossed the seas over to the continent of Africa.

When a new restaurant has even the slightest touch of Nobu Style, people will often say, "It's a bit like Nobu's." For me, that is the highest praise.

Many people asked me when I published my first cookbook, "What are you going to do if people copy these recipes that you worked so hard to create?" But I can't think of anything that could delight a chef more than to know that the dishes he or she created were being enjoyed worldwide. This is the way it should be. Besides, as I always tell them, "No problem. They can copy my recipes, but not my *kokoro* (heart)."

It would make me even happier if the chefs who copy me developed a good reputation and became stiff competition. The stimulation would be a great opportunity for me to grow. I know several people who were inspired by my example to become chefs and open their own restaurants. What could bring a chef greater happiness than this?

WHAT TO DO WITH THE REST OF MY LIFE

When you tackle new challenges and do your best, you reach a vantage point from which you can see new things and, from there, you can take another step forward. I have been doing this all my life. Now I travel the world as Nobuyuki Matsuhisa, visiting restaurants and meeting many people from whom I am always learning. I have even launched a hotel business. But I do not think my work is done yet. When I passed the age of sixty, I began thinking about the rest of my life. As I did so, the desire to teach everything I have learned to upcoming generations rose inside me. I became convinced that this is what I should now devote myself to doing. What made me feel this so strongly was Sakai, my best friend who literally saved my life.

I can still remember the day I entered high school and the moment I first met him. He was like a breath of fresh air. When it came to fashion, he could pull anything off and looked really cool in the Ivy League style so popular at the time. After graduating, he worked for a major construction company while continuing his studies, and then set up his own business once he received his certification as an architect. He often came to visit me at Matsuei-sushi in Shinjuku and joined me on my trips around Japan. Every time I failed in business overseas and returned home penniless, he was the one who came to my rescue. On the night my wife was in the hospital giving birth to our second child, he came and stayed with me and my daughter in our shabby one-room apartment. A friend in need is a friend indeed. For me, that friend was Sakai.

When Sakai got married, my wife and I arranged the whole thing at the famous Glass Church in Los Angeles. Although we were still quite poor, we felt that it was the least we could do and provided every hospitality we could think of. Matsuhisa went on to become a success, followed by Nobu, and I became very busy traveling around the world. Even so, whenever I went to Japan, I always called up Sakai. When we built our house, he arranged things with the construction company and went out of his way to help. The sushi counter at Matsuhisa in Los Angeles was ordered and assembled by Sakai. I knew that I could count on him to do things right. He was so efficient that we called him Sakai the Organizer, and he was always reliable. I really loved him; he was the very best of friends, and I owed him so much.

But one time when I called him from America, he seemed very curt. I wondered what he was upset about. In fact, he was so brusque that I was a bit offended. Several months later, I came back for New Year's and called him from the car on my way in from the airport. "How was your holiday?" I asked. "Did you go anywhere?" But again, his response seemed blunt and cold.

"Nope. No point," he said. "It's too crowded everywhere." I was annoyed and puzzled by his behavior.

Two days later, I received a call from his wife. She told me that Sakai had passed away. At first, I could not comprehend what she was saying. Struggling to control my shock, I left Tokyo immediately for their house in Saitama, the same house to which Sakai had welcomed me, my wife, and our baby for a few days on our return from South America. I stayed beside his body for some time. Then his wife led me into a separate room. There she told me that he had committed suicide. His business had run into trouble, and he had hanged himself at home. I was speechless.

THE IMMATURITY THAT BLINDED ME TO THE SUFFERING OF MY BEST FRIEND

Sakai had sounded brusque not because he was angry, but because he was in great pain. I had thought of him as my very best friend. He had saved me countless times. So why couldn't I see that he was really calling out for help? Why didn't I tell him, "Sakai, what's wrong? What happened? If there's anything I can do to help, just say so. I'd do anything for you." What made me feel the worst was that, when he was curt with me, I had actually thought, *What's wrong with you? Are you jealous or something?* I hated that part of myself.

I travel around the world telling people to think about others and imagine how they would feel if they were in the other person's position. So why couldn't I see how much Sakai, my closest friend, was suffering? Why couldn't I have said something kind to him? I felt wretched and ashamed, filled with remorse. To this day, I still feel tremendous pain. I cannot forgive myself.

As I stood there stunned, Sakai's wife handed me a scrapbook. She had always called her husband "Sakai-san," meaning "Mr. Sakai." "Sakai-san loved you so much," she told me. "He was always boasting about you. Whenever he heard that you were going to be on TV, he called up all his friends and told them. Whenever you were in the papers or a magazine, he would cut out the article and paste it in this scrapbook." The scrapbook was filled with articles, all neatly organized. Tears streamed down my face as I pictured him cutting them out and pasting them in.

I still remember his face as he lay in the coffin. Every year on the anniversary of his death, I visit the *bodaiji* temple to pray for his soul, but I will never be free from this pain. I should go to his house, offer incense, and speak with his wife, but I am too afraid. I know I should pick up my courage and go, but I haven't been able to bring myself to do it.

I lost the very best of friends.

When I was thinking of killing myself in Alaska, it was my wife and children who kept me going. When I returned to Japan, barely holding myself together emotionally, and was spurned by everyone I had known, Sakai was the only one who welcomed me back with open arms. Yet, when he was suffering so much that he could no longer bear to live, I couldn't help him. No, not *couldn't*. I *didn't* help him.

I am still dealing with that fact. I don't know when this pain will fade away. Maybe I will have to carry it for the rest of my life. Perhaps it's my homework. I never want to lose someone I love again. This thought has grown stronger ever since Sakai died. If I can, I want to make even one more person happy; I want to be there for the people I care about when they need me. I want this more than anything. I'm going to keep on trying so that when my time comes, I can cross the finish line and know that I did my very best, right to the end. As I am not a very sophisticated man, this is the only approach to life that I can think of.

WORKING AS HARD AS I CAN IS THE EASIEST WAY

Some people assume that I must have been born with a flair for cooking and an aptitude for artistic presentation. They think that this is the reason for my success. But I disagree. Neither Ichiro Suzuki nor Sadaharu Oh could have become top baseball stars through innate ability alone. They may have natural talent, but they also had to strive.

Many people tell me, "Nobu, you're so great," but I don't think so. I'm simply trying to do my best at all times. That's just who I am. For me, that's the easiest way. Just think about it. If you're always doing your best, you never need to make excuses. People who work hard are cool. People who give everything their best shot are forgiven when they make mistakes. As long as you keep trying as hard as you can, you will never regress. If you do your best, someone will always help you when you stumble and fall. You also never need to compare yourself with anyone else. You can just carry on doing your personal best.

I think this perspective stems, in large part, from my experience in Alaska when I was pushed to the brink of suicide. Even that dark despair was a lesson in life worth learning. I know that

I am very blessed to be in an environment where I can continue to strive. When I think about how that environment was created, I realize that it comes from focusing solely on my guests, not on money. I was able to forge ahead because the vector of my efforts never wavered. This is the source of my confidence.

I CAN STRIVE BECAUSE I'M A COWARD

I may have confidence, but I'm not going to press my luck. Part of me is still a coward because of the many hard knocks I experienced before establishing the first Matsuhisa. But I think that my timid nature has actually led to good results. It keeps me on my toes. If I started cutting corners, I could easily gravitate toward laziness. That thought terrifies me, and, because I am afraid, I work very hard. Although opening a new restaurant is scary, that fear forces me to focus fully on my work.

I think it's especially important to reaffirm my roots and stay true to myself when things are going smoothly. My fear strengthens my resolve to make sure I don't lose what I have built up so far. And that fear is rooted in my experience of losing everything in Alaska. Looking back on my life, I'm grateful that I was able to keep on striving. I became totally absorbed in my work, and this is where it has brought me. Now I am turning a fourth corner. How to get around that corner and make it to the finish line will be my theme from here on. Many people have helped me to reach this point. Now it is my turn to help others. That is where I want to use my money.

DON'T BOTHER AIMING TO BECOME A GLOBAL HUMAN RESOURCE

Japanese people talk about how globalization is beginning to affect their society, but in reality, I think that Japan is already part of a global society. Just look at the fact that English is now being taught in Japanese elementary schools. When I was a child, nobody would have dreamed that this would happen. It may take some time to see results, but as long as we continue to educate children to be more internationally minded, within ten or twenty years the elementary school children of today will have grown up equipped to work on the world stage.

I never received any education or training for working abroad or thinking globally. Yet I crossed the sea with nothing but my knife and flung myself into learning other languages, cultures, and values. And I like to think that I helped spread Japanese cuisine to other parts of the world in the process. It wasn't international awareness or foreign language ability that made this possible. Rather it was the fact that I never wavered in my convictions as a Japanese person. If you have conviction, your message will reach others.

Picking up a language is easy. Necessity will force you to learn. When we opened Nobu New York, I could not say a full sentence in English. Instead, I just strung together the words I knew. Yet, I still communicated. I was even interviewed for an English-learning program on Japan's national TV station as an example of being able to communicate despite having poor English.

So don't be afraid to leave home. Get out into the world. Instead of worrying about how to become internationally minded, just go ahead and try it. When you do, you will almost certainly hit a wall, but figuring out how to get yourself over that wall will give you the chance to grow. Once you have cleared it, you're bound to hit another, so just keep on climbing and growing. If you keep at it, the walls that rise up in front of you will gradually dwindle in size. I think this is what it means to live fully focused in the moment. As long as you do your very best, it doesn't matter if you are internationally minded or not. The road will always open before you.

PAYING IT FORWARD

I often encourage young people to choose the work they like without worrying about job conditions or social status. If you choose the path that calls, if you do the work you love, you will pour your passion into it and that will help you overcome any difficulties. The more hurdles you clear, the more confident you will become in your ability to clear them. The more you persevere, the smaller each new obstacle will appear. Whenever you aren't sure, trust your intuition. Instead of focusing on things like earnings or status, just choose the work that you feel you will enjoy. That is your compass.

If a certain path feels right, take it. You can always change direction if you realize along the way that it was not the right choice. As long as you have passion, no detour is painful. As long as you live your life to the fullest, results will always come. Even if you fail, someone will always help you if they see that you are sincerely doing your best. I was able to come this far thanks to the help of many people along the way. That is why I want to help others as much as I can. I want to repay the kindness of those who helped me when I was young by extending the same support to upcoming generations. Sometimes that kindness may be betrayed. Sometimes I may be deceived. But I would rather be deceived than deceive others.

IN THE END, IT ALL COMES DOWN TO PASSION

What I really want to share with young people is not cooking skills or the art of communication, but something that can be summed up in a single word—passion. As I mentioned before, I think that a person can only truly be considered a master of their trade when they can pass on their passion to the next generation.

Although I dreamed of becoming a sushi chef and of working overseas from my youth, I never imagined that restaurants around the world, and even hotels, would one day bear my name. This was simply the result of hard work and my passionate desire to make my guests smile. I am a very happy man, but if you asked me what the secret to happiness is, I could not tell you. Because you can only understand life by living it for yourself. You will never find the answer without making your own efforts. Of course you will make mistakes, but these will teach you important lessons. All I can tell you is to stay passionate. That is the only rule for happiness that I know.

WHAT IF WE ALL TRIED TO SEE THINGS FROM THE OTHER'S PERSPECTIVE?

Not everyone can see life like this right from the start. Many people feel lost and bewildered when they hit a wall. I have thought about this a lot, ever since Sakai died. That's why I believe we should consciously do our best to be considerate and supportive of each other, particularly of our close family, friends, and coworkers. This is important because we're part of the same "team."

To be considerate requires imagination, the ability to intuit what the other person is feeling. If everyone tried to be considerate, we would all speak with greater kindness to each other. If everyone in the world made a conscious effort to do this, there

Nobu in the Cape Town kitchen.

would be no more wars. I believe that the way individuals interact is cumulative and affects the way nations interact. This may
sound like an exaggeration, but it's quite true.

People of many nationalities work at Nobu. Miscommu-
nication often occurs due to cultural differences. Our menu is
based on Japanese cuisine, but that cuisine may inadvertently
end up being Thai cuisine with Japanese elements when a Thai
chef cooks it. What a Japanese person recognizes with one bite is
not easily communicated to others. The only solution is to keep
working together and to keep communicating. It was through
such constant and daily effort that Nobu teamwork developed.

In March 2014, I celebrated my birthday in Perth, Australia.
A Korean staff member gave me a present with the words "For
Nobu-san." These kinds of connections give me hope. Even if
relations between countries like Japan and Korea should deterio-
rate, we can help to restore them through building such personal
friendships.

What if I were that person . . . When we pursue this thought
to perfection in our work, a single piece of sushi has the power to
touch a person's heart. I have proven that this attitude can eventually spread worldwide. The consideration shown by each one
of us really does change the world.

It is effort and perseverance that make the impossible possible. It is only by trying that we actually realize what we are capable of doing. I think that this is what it means to be human. If

we keep moving forward, even a millimeter a day, we are bound to achieve good results at some point. We have done well if we can say in the end that we're glad we did our best. I have been through a lot, but for me, to have reached this understanding is the greatest happiness.

Afterword

One day, a cassette tape arrived at Nobu Tokyo from a Japanese radio station. It was a recording of a program featuring the actor Ken Takakura. The purpose of the program was to introduce Japanese people who had achieved success overseas. Apparently, Ken chose to talk about me after reading an article in the magazine *Fujinkoron* entitled, "The Man Who Made Robert De Niro Wait Four Years." During the program, he remarked, "Nobu didn't *make* De Niro wait. I think De Niro *chose* to wait four years."

This comment really moved me and I wanted to get in touch with him. He had come to Matsuhisa once, just after it opened, but I never dreamed that he would introduce me on the radio. On the same program, he had also mentioned Sushizen, a restaurant in Hokkaido. I looked them up and then went all the way to Hokkaido to meet the owner, Tsutomu Shimamiya, at his restaurant. He was a little older than me. When I explained what I wanted, he connected us, and Ken came to meet me at Hotel Okura in Tokyo.

This meeting was the beginning of our friendship. I took him a wooden Buddha carved by Yoshizaki, my old friend from high school. I had given one to De Niro as a gift, too. Ken was thrilled and even wrote about it in a magazine. Clearly, he had a strong faith. He once gave me a bell for the Buddhist altar in our home and had an artisan he knew carve our family crest on it. He also gave me a small sword custom-made by a swordsmith as a protective charm when my first grandchild was born.

Ken actually delivered the bell in person, arriving unannounced at our door. I invited him in for tea, but he refused, saying, "Today, I just came to say hello."

"Well, then, next time be sure to call me before you come," I said.

The next time he called before he came, just as I had asked. "I'm going to drop by with a DVD," he said.

"Great. Where are you now?" I asked.

"Downstairs," he answered.

"You know, Ken, when I said call me before you come, I meant . . ." That was such a Ken Takakura thing to do.

It's the same when he comes to the restaurant. He'll phone and say, "Nobu, I'm on my way."

"Where are you?" I'll ask.

"Out front."

Ken always tells me, "Nobu, you're amazing. You've done a great job, you know." When he first talked about me on that radio program, our business had not grown as big as it is now. When Nobu restaurants began spreading around the world, he said to me, "You see, Nobu, I was right about you." He's a very kind man. I phone him every month when I visit Japan. Recently, however, I was away for two months instead of one. When I called him, he said, "Oh, I'm so glad you called." He had been worried because he hadn't heard from me.

Ken has a good sense of humor. When I first learned how to send emails by cell phone, I sent him one as a joke. He called me up and said, "Sorry. I don't know how to send emails." I kept emailing him just for fun, and then one day, he emailed me back with, "Thank you." He phoned me right after and said, "Emailing's kind of fun, isn't it?" Now he sometimes emails me when I leave messages on his phone.

He loves movies and often talks about them. When I call him, he'll tell me about the movies he's watched recently and what he thought of them. He thoughtfully sends me DVDs of any movies in which I seem interested. If I happen to be in Tokyo at the time, he'll drive all the way to my house to deliver them in person. He also sent me many DVDs of the movies he has starred in, and I like to watch these when I have time to relax at home.

He's a big fan of De Niro. He gave De Niro and me matching watches. In his office, De Niro had a large copy of a photo of himself from a scene in the movie *Raging Bull*. I asked him if he would let me have it so that I could give it to Ken. De Niro, who also knows Ken, made a copy and even signed it. When I gave this to him, Ken looked very impressed. "Nobu," he said, "this is amazing. How did he copy such a big photo?"

I really look up to Ken. We've had some long talks, and every time we do, I am struck once again by what a great human being he is, and particularly by his humility. I am amazed by how purehearted he remains even though he is over eighty. There is so much I have to learn from him. Just talking with him makes me more sincere and genuine, as if I am returning to the roots of who I am. He's seventeen years older than me, and when I look at his upright figure, I think that if I do my best, I should be okay for the next seventeen years. I think that very few people demonstrate such qualities as Ken does.

I'm sure that many people flock around him, but the fact that despite this he trusts me enough to share his thoughts on so many things makes me very happy and gives me great confidence. I respect him more than anyone I know. Looking at him makes me want to try harder. It made me so proud when he wrote a comment for the first cookbook I ever published. With a pure and simple heart, I will keep striving to follow his example in my own profession, spreading Nobu Style Japanese cuisine, which makes people around the world happy.

In closing, I would like to express my heartfelt gratitude to my father, who died when I was young, to my family, and to all those who have taught and supported me throughout my life. It is thanks to them that I have become who I am.

Nobuyuki Matsuhisa
May 2014, aboard a plane on the way to
prepare for the opening of Matsuhisa Paris

———————————————————————

Ever since my memoir was published in Japanese in 2014, people have been telling me that they'd really like to read it in English. Although it has taken three years, I'm pleased to be able to share with you the English version.

In 2016, a new Matsuhisa restaurant opened in Paris followed by one in Denver and another in Munich, while a Nobu restaurant opened in Newport Beach. Nobu Hotels have opened in Manila in the Philippines as well as in Miami and London with more scheduled to open in Marbella and Ibiza Bay, Spain, and in Riyadh, Saudi Arabia. The sixteen-room Nobu Ryokan also opened in Malibu Beach. At the end of 2016, the Nobu restaurant in Waikiki moved and reopened as Nobu Honolulu, while the first Nobu in New York just moved to the Financial District in May 2017.

Although our restaurant and hotel businesses continue to expand, what I do hasn't changed. I continue to travel for ten months of the year visiting Nobu and Matsuhisa restaurants around the world. The number has increased to the point where I can no longer get to all of them once a year, but I love it when chefs and staff that I haven't seen for over ten months pepper me with questions, as if they are determined not to miss this opportunity. For me, being able to offer support and to witness people's growth like this is a source of joy and motivation.

On a personal level, the biggest difference between now and three years ago is the fact that Ken Takakura is no longer here in this world. I will never meet or talk with him again. He passed away in November 2014, just three months after this memoir was published in Japanese. Even now when I think of him, my eyes fill with tears. At least I have the comfort of knowing that he read my book. He always told me, "Nobu, you've got a great smile," so I'm glad to see a photo of me smiling on the cover of this book.

It also gives me comfort to know that I was able to bring Ken and De Niro together. I had been friends with Ken for more than ten years and had invited him to come two or three times when De Niro was visiting Japan, but the timing didn't work out. About a year before Ken died, however, I invited him again when De Niro was visiting. He phoned me back and said, "Nobu, I'll just drop in for ten minutes."

De Niro arrived a little early. When Ken appeared, all he ordered was an espresso while De Niro had a meal and sake. The two of them began talking with my daughter Junko interpreting. Neither of them was very talkative, but once they got started on movies, they couldn't stop. I could see how much they respected each other as movie people. Ken's ten minutes lasted over an hour and a half. Occasionally, I would ask him if he would like something to eat, but he declined each time because he had said at the beginning, "Just espresso." That was so like him. He looked really happy that night.

In his tribute for Ken's memorial service, De Niro wrote about this meeting, and the knowledge that I had managed to bring these two together warmed my heart.

With a prayer for the repose of Ken's soul, I lay down my pen.

Nobuyuki Matsuhisa
June 2017, aboard a plane on the way to Ibiza Bay, Spain

12/17